# Exemplification in Communication

## The Influence of Case Reports
## on the Perception of Issues

## LEA's COMMUNICATION SERIES
### Jennings Bryant / Dolf Zillmann, General Editors

For a complete list of titles in LEA's Communication Series, please contact Lawrence Erlbaum Associates, Publishers

# Exemplification in Communication

## The Influence of Case Reports
## on the Perception of Issues

Dolf Zillmann
*University of Alabama*

and

Hans-Bernd Brosius
*University of Munich*

LAWRENCE ERLBAUM ASSOCIATES, PUBLISHERS

2000 Mahwah, New Jersey London

Lawrence Erlbaum Associates, Inc., Publishers
10 Industrial Avenue
Mahwah, NJ 07430

Cover design by Kathryn Houghtaling Lacey

**Library of Congress Cataloging-in-Publication Data**

Zillmann, Dolf.
Exemplification in communication : the influence of case re-
ports on the perception of issues / Dolf Zillmann and
Hans-Bernd Brosius.
p. cm.
Includes bibliographical references and index.
ISBN 0-8058-2810-9 (cloth : alk. paper)
ISBN 0-8058-2811-7 (pbk.: alk. paper)
1. Communication. 2. Example. I. Brosius, Hans-Bernd.
II. Title.
P91 .Z54 2000
302.2 —dc21                                              99-086796
                                                             cip

Books published by Lawrence Erlbaum Associates are printed
on acid-free paper, and their bindings are chosen for strength
and durability.

Printed in the United States of America
10  9  8  7  6  5  4  3  2  1

# Contents

# Preface

Exemplification is fundamental to the perception of phenomena of the so-called real world. As segments of pertinent experience that are stored in memory, exemplars provide samplings of information about past occurrences that foster dispositions and ultimately direct behavior toward similar occurrences on later encounter. A limited number of experiences thus serve as the basis for judging a larger body of similar occurrences. The implicit generalization amounts to a spontaneously executed inductive inference. Inferences of this kind are made by all species capable of adaptation through learning. Humans, no doubt, have made these inferences through the millennia, and they are still making them, routinely so and nonconsciously for the most part.

The reliance on exemplification by primary experience has, of course, not appreciably changed for nonhuman species. For humans, in contrast, it has been enormously complicated. With the refinement of communication skills, especially with the emergence of linguistic competencies, the pertinent experiences of others became communicable, and phenomena had to be judged by integrating primary experiences with communicatively conveyed ones. This broadening of the experiential base is obviously advantageous in enabling individuals to judge phenomena laying outside the bounds of their own limited and thus limiting experience. It came at a cost, however. Experiences related by others could be self-serving, inadvertently erroneous, or deliberately deceptive, forcing individuals to be on guard about others' communicative intentions.

This principal condition exists for communication by media institutions as much as it pervades direct interpersonal communication, even more so because any misinformation disseminated by the media impacts vast numbers of people. Some institutions, such as the entertainment industry, claim poetic license and reject any responsibility for effects that their exemplifications might have. Supported by the intuition of numerous communication scholars, specifically their contention that "people know better" than to let themselves be influenced by fiction, this industry is not held accountable for misrepresentations that may foster misperceptions. However, no such license is given to media institutions that are dedicated to providing, and that purport to furnish, veridical and reliable accounts of phenomena of consequence for their audiences, potentially for the citizenry at large. Of these media institutions, the news in print, in broadcast, and in computer format, along with newslike educational efforts also irrespective of means of delivery, are of central importance.

The news media thrive on exemplification. The case report, or more accurately, the aggregation of intriguing case reports, as it appears to hold considerable public interest, may be considered the lifeblood of journalism. Accounts of societally relevant phenomena thus tend to be conveyed by samplings of cases. Such samplings are usually composed of arbitrarily extracted special cases. The focus is mostly on extraordinary rather than on typical cases. The samplings, therefore, are selective cases that do not impartially represent the population of cases that define particular phenomena. The likely result of this partial, nonrepresentative accounting is the inaccurate perception, if not the plain misperception, of the projected phenomena.

The exemplification of phenomena is, of course, often supplemented by more general descriptions. Specifications may include measured and quantified assessments. They may convey data that are collected in adherence to the principles of science. Particular manifestations of a phenomenon may be distinguished in terms of any number of criteria, for instance, and their absolute and relative incidence can then be determined. Information of this kind has been labeled *base-rate information*. It often accompanies exemplifications, and it is generally considered to be less partial and hence more reliable than the information provided by selective exemplars. On occasion, such information gives impetus to news reports. On other occasions, it is furnished to correct presumed erroneous perceptions from biased exemplification.

Irrespective of the reasons for including base-rate information in the projection of phenomena, however, the issue of misperception from exposure to admixtures of selective exemplification and potentially more reliable base-rate information is defined by the reception of these messages. How will recipients process the information? Will they base their perception of issues primarily on the display of exemplars? This can be expected on grounds of the built-in heuristics that ensured the survival of the species. Additionally, will recipients absorb the comparatively abstract base-rate information, process it carefully, and use it to correct false impressions invited by inappropriate exemplar aggregations? Those who believe in the careful digestion of news reports may expect that base-rate information has this power to put exemplars in their place as mere illustrations, thereby depriving them of undue influence. On the other hand, the processing of less concrete, more abstract information may be considered evolutionarily too vernal to be capable of overpowering the impressions based on the deep-rooted mechanisms of extrapolating tacit knowledge of a population of cases from a handful of actually known ones. Of particular interest are the delayed consequences of the provision of concrete versus abstract information. Are incidence rates and the like as well retained as concrete cases, not to mention extraordinary concrete cases? If not, should it not be expected that the influence of base-rate information on the perception of issues will diminish more rapidly than that of exemplification, ultimately allowing the exemplar influence to become increasingly dominant?

Obviously, these concerns cannot be resolved on intuitive grounds alone. Empirical exploration and clarification is a necessity. Resolution in these terms is, of course, the primary objective of the experimental work reported in this volume.

Our treatise on exemplification in communication commences with a detailed conceptual examination of the relationship between limited sets of exemplars and the consequent perception of the exemplified population of occurrences. The focus is on exemplifications that are likely to foster accurate and reliable perceptions of the exemplified population, as well as on those associated with varying degrees of risk of causing misperceptions. This examination not only provides theoretical guidelines for reliable exemplification but also explores the interface between direct and mediated experience in the assessment of issues.

Chapter 2 addresses the professional practice of exemplifying in various domains of communication. De facto exemplification is detailed for both print and broadcast news. Attention is also given to exemplification in advertising and in forms of fictional exposition.

In chapter 3, the prevalent psychological theories pertaining to impression formation and issue perception are outlined. They are applied to exemplification specifically, and their usefulness in this context is discerned. Of focal interest are the heuristic paradigms of information processing. Emotional reactivity to exemplars in the mediation of issue perception is also given much consideration.

Chapter 4 summarizes the relevant research, mostly experimental investigations, concerning the influence on issue perception of exemplars and of base-rate information presented in the news. The research demonstrations reveal, among other things, remarkable effects of various exemplar–counterexemplar distributions, qualitative exemplar distortions, emotion-inducing exemplars, threat-conveying pictorial exemplars, and even innocuous and seemingly incidentally employed pictorial exemplars. Base-rate information emerges as a relatively powerless qualifier. The time course of these effects on issue perception also receives scrutiny.

In chapter 5, the effects of de facto exemplification in fiction and in quasi-fiction are examined. The results of both correlational and experimental investigations are integrated to assess influences on issue perception. As this exposition is secondary to the interest in exemplification consequences of news consumption, it is discussed to establish that fiction and quasi-fiction can have and do have discernible effects on issue perception. The coverage of research is eclectic and not exhaustive, however.

The concluding chapter, finally, addresses media literacy specific to exemplification. Recommendations are derived from the reported body of research. The recommendations are separated for information providers and for information consumers. Specifically, journalists are informed of presentational strategies and the likely interpretation of particular exemplifications in the interest of fostering correct issue perception in recipients—or at least, of minimizing misperception. The recipients, on the other hand, are informed about defensive strategies that they can pursue in order to minimize misinterpretations. They are alerted to presentational features that invite misperception, and they are encouraged to discount information presented in particular ways. The possibility of perceptual effects of fiction and of quasi-fiction is considered in this context, and measures to guard against inappropriate influence are indicated.

The authors have to confess to a long-standing common interest in exemplification and its consequences for people living in so-called rich media environments. Teaching research seminars in the mid-1980s at Indiana University, Dolf Zillmann started to be intrigued with this phenomenon. However, the cursory interest consolidated to a genuine research interest only later, especially during the presence of Hans-Bernd Brosius as a post-doctoral research associate at the University of Alabama in 1990. At this time, the authors pondered the issue and decided to explore it. But as Brosius had to return to the University of Mainz in Germany, the exploration proceeded rather independently. The result, nonetheless, is a program of complementary investigations that were conducted at the University of Alabama, and the Universities of Mainz and Munich, Germany, the latter being the institution with which Brosius has been affiliated since 1996. The research of this program constitutes, of course, the core of the present treatise on exemplification.

It is by no means implied that we conducted our research alone and in isolation. We greatly benefited from the competent work of numerous collaborators. We owe a great debt of gratitude, in fact, to many of our assistants as well as to former students and colleagues. Also deserving of our gratitude are the thousands of participants in our investigations. The reported research could not have been done without the contributions of all these parties. Last but not least, we are deeply grateful to our wives for encouraging and comforting us when the task at hand seemed overwhelming.

—*Dolf Zillmann*
—*Hans-Bernd Brosius*

# ONE

# Exemplification in Communication

Everybody is familiar with examples. Everybody has been given examples, and everybody has related examples to others in efforts of elucidating a broader concept or issue. Everybody, then, has some tacit understanding of a relation between an example and a larger entity to be exemplified by it. What is implied is that more than one example exists and that several examples tend to do a better job than just one in explaining aspects and features of the exemplified entity. What is also implied is that an utterly unique, singular incident, such as the first moon landing by humans, could only exemplify itself; hence, it could not serve as an example of other first moon landings by humans. It may, however, serve as an example of other landings of spacecraft, if the expositional focus were on aspects of the event that exhibit a degree of similarity with other events under consideration.

Tacit understanding of exemplification thus entails recognition of shared features between an example (also called *exemplum* or *exemplar*) and the exemplified, as well as between all possible examples (also called *exempla* or *exemplars*) of the exemplified. In simple terms, such sharing amounts to similarity between exemplars and the exemplified. Lexical definitions focus on this similarity by stipulating that the exemplar be typical or characteristic of exemplified entities. The highest degree of similarity is demanded by definitions that specify the exemplar as a case in point or an instance of the exemplified entities. Both specifications suggest an array of identical entities from which any single one can be taken to exemplify all others. Each and every instance may be singled out to inform about all other instances.

The stipulation that all exemplars be identical may seem overly stringent but actually is not when one considers that the stipulation need not be applied to all features of an entity. We can speak of New Yorkers as identical entities in that their domicile is New York. They may differ in any other regard. It is important, then, to distinguish a set of features for which interexemplar similarity is required from a set of features that are free to vary. The latter features are immaterial in considering a particular instance an exemplar of other instances subsumed in the exemplified group of instances. As a consequence, exemplars are to be considered instances of whatever kind that are capable of representing other instances only to the extent that they share with them all defining features.

The specification that exemplifying and exemplified instances may be of whatever kind needs elaboration. The features of perceptible entities and events obviously can be represented to percipients. Features of objects such as trees, houses, and bridges can be exemplified, as can dogs, people, and computers, along with their perceivable actions. The overt "behavior" of entities is, of course, ready subject to exemplification. Less obvious might be the representation of abstractions and concepts that elude direct perceptual control. Extracted relations between entities, either in the form of covariations or causality, may be exemplified nonetheless. Similarly, the match between intent and performance, or that between precept, action choice, the expectation of consequences, and actual consequences may also be exemplified. For instance, children who consume a fair amount of fairy tales readily appreciate that elderly women with a deformity of the back and a screechy voice harbor hostile intentions and, given the opportunity, act on them. These children also appreciate that actions, such as a witch's efforts to make a meal of Hansel and Gretel, are in violation of moral precepts and call for punishment. Moreover, they are able to spot a match between punitive precepts and punitive actions against a wrongdoer and hence can rejoice when the witch gets her just deserts. All of these assessments and judgments are exemplars of conduct—in particular, of socially reproached and punished conduct as well as of socially approved and rewarded conduct.

The illustration of witch-defining features entails a leap from detecting an abstraction to applying it to other situations and contexts. This extension is part and parcel of exemplification. If the identification of an exemplar in a given context (i.e., the recognition of a resemblance between a familiar abstraction and a particular manifestation of that abstraction) were the terminal stage of the process, exemplification would be of little relevance to communication. As it stands, however, exemplification is mostly the starting point in that the world of exemplars appears to influence our perception and judgment of essentially all phenomena and issues of the so-called real world.

Analogous to forming impressions and dispositions toward entities and happenings on a sampling of pertinent experiences, our perception and judgment of phenomena and issues with which we have little or no immediate contact are bound to be influenced by samplings of mediated events. Such influence can be seen as the result of nonconscious inductive inference (Bargh, 1996; Kissin, 1986; Lewicki, 1986). The more general case is inferred on the basis of limited mediated experience with relevant happenings. For the vast majority of the citizenry, for instance, violent crime is not immediately experienced. Yet perceptions are formed on the basis of news reports, friends' hearsay, and possibly fictional portrayals. Moreover, judgments of the moral variety are formed on the basis of these perceptions. We may smile or cringe when a child, apparently as the result of frequent witch exemplification in Grimm-style fairy tales, points to a lady in the street and utters, "A witch, a witch!" However, do we routinely, if ever, examine the etiology of our own beliefs and dispositions, especially regarding the likely influence of communication-mediated exemplars? Surprisingly little attention has been paid to this aspect of interpersonal and media influence.

We attempt to correct this neglect by subjecting the influence of communication-mediated exemplification to systematic analysis. We first examine exemplification in conceptual terms, then ascertain what the media do in generating an exemplar flood, and finally explore the effects of exemplification on the perception and judgment of phenomena and issues.

## CONCEPTUAL CONSIDERATIONS

In conveying information about the flow of happenings in the so-called real world it always has been deemed appropriate, if it was not plainly recognized as a necessity, to cut this flow into manageable chunks and to isolate and focus on some events at the expense of attention to occurrences in between (Burns, 1992; Rosch & Lloyd, 1978; Tversky & Hemenway, 1984). Narratives, as a rule, leap from event to event, irrespective of the events' locality and position in time. More important here, narration aggregates events that exhibit sufficient phenomenal similarity to warrant their being classified as manifestations of the same kind. Such grouping implies that each and every grouped event, to the extent that it shares all essential attributes with the remaining grouped events, is capable of representing the group at large—meaning that it is capable of providing reliable information about all other events in this group and thus about the group itself. It is this capacity of individual events that defines them as *exemplars* of an event group. Given that the events in a particular group share all essential attributes, as was stipulated, each and every group member would indeed *exemplify* the group attributes. If, for instance, it can be considered established that all humans are mortal, then each and every human would exemplify human mortality.

The outlined paradigm of *representation* is, of course, an abstraction. Since antiquity it has been argued that no two events are truly alike. Grouping, classifying, or categorizing on grounds of likeness has been practiced through the ages nonetheless (Burns, 1992; B. Hayes-Roth & Hayes-Roth, 1977; Mervis & Rosch, 1981). Economy and efficiency of thought and of information conveyance would seem to necessitate it. It should be clear, however, that conditions in which grouped events are fully interchangeable, and thus capable of representing the group without error, exist rarely, if ever. Especially in the realm of human affairs, exemplification is bound to be less than perfect, and a certain degree of imprecision is unavoidable and also may be immaterial for many practical purposes.

The indicated imprecision, formally expressed, derives from the fact that events are necessarily grouped on the basis of a limited number of attributes, with a potentially large number of additional attributes remaining unidentified or being ignored. If $n$ attributes are identified and employed as grouping criteria, $m$ attributes may vary freely. For instance, if the group event is defined as carjacking committed in the United States during the 1990 to 1996 period by men aged 15 to 25 years, any particular carjacking within this group is likely to exemplify the specified crimes only poorly because some perpetrators will have only threatened violence, whereas others may have used force, even deadly force, against the evicted car owner. Exemplification of the crime by any particular crime thus cannot fully and impartially represent the grouped crimes.

Conceptually, precision in exemplification is readily specified. It requires that $n$, the number of defined attributes employed as grouping criteria, be associated with $m = 0$, the number of undefined attributes that may be pertinent. In case it is recognized that $m > 0$, $m$ must be reduced to zero by incorporating the $m$ attributes in $n$. In the carjacking illustration, this would mean that subgroups should be created and that exemplification should be limited to these subgroups. For instance, the group of deadly carjackings would have to be isolated and could be exemplified only by individual cases of deadly carjackings. Carjackings by other means would have to be treated analogously. Such group partitioning by increased definitional specificity would be recursive without apparent end. In the carjacking illustration, deadly force may, after all, have been applied in different ways; for instance, by clubbing, by knifing, or by shooting. The number of grouping attributes would have to be increased again, producing an ever larger number of ever smaller, yet more specific, event groups. The direct, single-case exemplification of the crime of carjacking irrespective of particular manifestations would no longer be feasible because the subgroups, unless their case count is zero in all but one of the groups, are bound to reveal marked differences in the manifestations of the grouped events. Depending on one's focal interest, then, it will have to be allowed that $m$, the number of undefined and uncontrolled attributes, be larger than zero. Variation in these attributes will have to be accepted on grounds of practicality, meaning that some degree of imprecision in exemplification is to be tolerated in order to achieve greater efficiency in the conveyance of information about grouped events.

Although some imprecision in exemplification may be unavoidable, the concept of representation implies that the highest degree of precision attainable under given circumstances should be pursued. Common definitions of exemplification stipulate that a group of events need to be represented by single events that are typical and characteristic of the group. Exemplification by atypical and uncharacteristic events is deemed inappropriate because it fails to provide reliable information about the group. The arbitrary selection of "a case in point" can have utility only for the exemplification of a homogeneous event group; that is, for a group with minimal variance in uncontrolled attributes. Whenever such variance is more than minimal, which it is likely to be for most issues of concern, exemplification by arbitrary selection would seem to be unacceptable—even irresponsible, if the object is to provide veridical information about an event group.

For instance, if carjackings with deadly outcome amounted to a trivial number and noninjurious outcomes accounted for almost all crimes of this kind, it would seem inappropriate, indeed, to exemplify the crime of carjacking by the presentation of a deadly case only. Such inappropriate exemplification is bound to mislead the recipient of the information, resulting in erroneous conceptions about the danger associated with the crime at large.

The obvious limitations of exemplification by a case in point (i.e., one case) can be overcome, of course, by exemplification that draws on multiple exemplars. Using several or numerous exemplars does not guarantee greater precision in representation, however. Arbitrary selection of exemplars may lead to duplications of partiality and may thereby escalate misrepresentation. The selection of two or three deadly cases in our carjacking illustration should make that point. Representational accuracy would be better served if exemplars were selected blindly. In our illustration, the most frequently occurring forms of carjacking would likely be drawn to represent the crime, and greater accuracy would be insured, to a point. The frequent case, it should be noticed, defines what is to be considered typical and characteristic. If carjacking, for instance, is mostly injury-free, this attribute is typical and characteristic. Exemplification by a small number of blindly drawn exemplars, say three or five, would bring out this property of carjacking. It would furnish a reliable projection of the crime of carjacking in these terms. However, exemplification would probably not include deadly carjackings because of their extremely low incidence. Representation by a small number of blindly drawn exemplars thus may still be considered imperfect. It is likely to be incomplete, thereby allowing or fostering erroneous assessments of the grouped events. Only the use of large numbers of exemplars would insure the inclusion of infrequently occurring but nonetheless relevant events. Clearly, representational accuracy for a large event group is higher, the more closely the number of blindly drawn exemplifying events approximates the total of grouped events. However, although the employment of such large numbers of exemplars accomplishes great representational precision, it is often or mostly unworkable because it entails a forbidding amount of redundant information about the typical case. In our illustration, the recipient of an account of carjacking might have to be informed about hundreds of frequent cases before being appraised of the fact that carjacking may have deadly outcomes as well.

An apparent way out of this dilemma is, of course, to attach quantitative information to specific exemplars. The typicality of particular occurrences within a group of events would be defined in frequencies or in proportions. The effectiveness of such presentational strategies in terms of acquisition, processing, retention, and retrieval of the supplied information by recipients remains to be seen, however.

## DEFINITION OF THE
## EXEMPLIFICATION PROCESS

Our introductory comments may have made apparent that the representation of a group of events by exemplar events resembles that of the representation of a population of events by a sample of events. The relation between exemplification and sampling is indeed strong enough to accept the representation of population events by sampled events as a model for some forms of exemplification. We do, in fact, adopt much of the well-established nomenclature and procedures of statistical representation and inference for particular types of exemplification. However, there exist forms of exemplification that differ considerably from the statistical model, and we modify this model as the circumstances require.

We first formalize exemplification processes that are analogous to sampling from a specified population and thereafter consider exemplifications that define populations.

### Exemplification of Known Event Populations

A *population* of events is defined as a usually finite aggregate of events that share a limited number of specified characteristics but that may differ in numerous unspecified properties.

A *sample* of events is defined as any possible subset of the population events.

A *random sample* of events is defined as any subset of the population events for which every sampled event had the same chance of inclusion. This is the condition of *equiprobability* that insures impartial, unbiased representation of the population by the sample.

A *subpopulation* of events is defined as a subset or a stratum of the population of events. Events subsumed in subsets or in strata are specified by a limited number of characteristics in addition to those specifying the events of the population. Sampling from a subpopulation is analogous to sampling from a population.

In the special case of complementary subpopulations of known size, samples drawn randomly from the subpopulations may be combined in proportion to their size to represent the population. This process, known as *stratified sampling*, is economical in that it prevents redundant oversampling in large subpopulations while insuring consideration of small subpopulations.

These concepts apply directly to the exemplification of well-defined, known populations and subpopulations of events. A minor adjustment concerns population size. Regarding exemplification, the mathematical abstraction of nonfinite, indefinitely large populations (that serves the estimation of a quantified property of events under consideration) has no utility and is unnecessary. Populations known through direct or through recorded observation are by definition of finite size. Moreover, known populations are not imagined ones but are presumed to have been measured in some fashion (i.e., in terms of defining attributes and of size).

Acceptance of these modifications allows the usage of the established statistical concepts in specifying the conditions of impartial exemplification of known populations and subpopulations of events. An exemplar is, of course, nothing other than an event subsumed in a population or subpopulation. Regarding human affairs, population events of concern are also referred to as *issues*. For instance, all cases of melanoma from excessive sun exposure define a health issue. Likewise, all cases of illiteracy define a relevant social issue. However, judgmental matters such as the perceived quality of wine from the last harvest or the appropriateness of using cellular phones in fine dining establishments also constitute issues.

We are now in a position to specify the conditions for the impartial exemplification of known, empirically established issues.

1. Issues defined by a known event population are impartially represented by any number of exemplars that are randomly selected from this population.

2. The precision of representation is a joint function of unspecified and hence uncontrolled variation of characteristics within the exemplars and of the number of exemplars. Specifically, representational precision decreases with the number of uncontrolled characteristics and increases with the number of exemplars. As a consequence, impartial exemplification is best achieved by increasing the number of randomly selected exemplars as the number of uncontrolled exemplar attributes increases.

For instance, if persons who caused accidents by driving recklessly define a social issue, exemplification of their population with a small number of exemplars might prove inadequate because numerous relevant characteristics would go unrepresented. Random selection might yield three young men—one Black, two White. Persons of other age, gender, and ethnicity would not be represented, nor would be conditions such as personality and habits pertinent to dangerous driving. Employment of a larger number of exemplars would offer some degree of protection against misrepresentation by the likely inclusion of these variables. Small exemplar numbers are adequate only under conditions where uncontrolled variance is minimal or immaterial. Representation by a single exemplar can be adequately representative only if the uncontrolled variation of characteristics is nil.

3. The precision of representation can be increased by the division of the population into subpopulations of known size. After subdivision by specified characteristics, three procedures can be employed. (a) Analogous to stratified sampling, in *stratified exemplification* a comparatively small number of exemplars is drawn from all subpopulations, with the size of these subpopulations as associated indicators of the prevalence and typicality of events in the subpopulations. (b) Alternatively, the proportions defined by the size of all subpopulations of the population of events are used as a guide in drawing specific numbers of exemplars from all subpopulations. Large subpopulations, then, are represented by large numbers of exemplars, and small subpopulations are represented by small numbers of exemplars. Extremely small subpopulations define a limiting condition. Their representation in such *proportional exemplification* may require excessively large numbers of exemplars representing large subpopulations. The indicated redundancy could be eliminated only by foregoing the exemplification of extremely small subpopulations. (c) Finally, an admixture of both procedures may be used to overcome the limitations of proportional exemplification. That is, proportional exemplification is employed initially. If it yields unmanageable redundancy for large proportions or no representation for minuscule ones, the proportion is conveyed along with the disproportional number of exemplars that amounts to under- or overrepresentation, respectively.

Figure 1.1 shows extremely selective exemplifications that yield misrepresentations. Figure 1.2 gives an overview of exemplification strategies that provide unbiased representations.

In terms of the reckless driver illustration, stratified exemplification would have involved segregation of the population by age, by gender, and/or by ethnicity. The absolute or relative size of the resulting subpopulations would have been indicated in connection with an arbitrary number of exemplars from each subpopulation. In proportional exemplification, by contrast, the size ratio of each subpopulation to the population would have been used to select exemplar numbers that are proportional with each subpopulation's size. Only if, as has been discussed, redundancy is deemed intolerable, or if nonrepresentation results, would proportionality be indexed by means other than the relative number of exemplars.

All of these exemplification strategies (i.e., 3a, 3b, and 3c) are superior to random exemplification of the population at large in that they inform about the events in subpopulations (i.e., events that otherwise are left undefined), and in that impartial representation of the population of events is achieved with fewer exemplars; that is, with lesser presentational investment as well as with lesser processing effort for the information recipient. Stratified and proportional exemplification would make clear, for instance, that the subpopulation of men entails more reck-

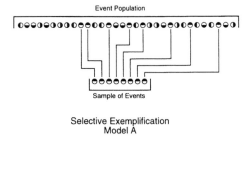

Event Population

Sample of Events

Selective Exemplification
Model A

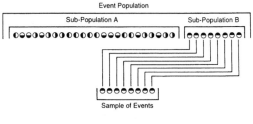

Event Population

Sub-Population A                    Sub-Population B

Sample of Events

Selective Exemplification
Model B

FIG. 1.1   Schemata of selective exemplification. (A) From a finite population of events that vary along four attributes, a sample of events characterized by just one of the four attributes is arbitrarily drawn. The population at large is misrepresented. If the events were carjackings in which the victim is either killed, badly injured, slightly injured, or not injured, the selection of carjackings with deadly outcomes obviously would not provide a fair representation of all carjackings. (B) The event population is separated into a subpopulation in which events characterized by only one specific attribute are singled out and a subpopulation in which events are characterized by the remaining three attributes. Essentially, a selectively drawn sample is declared a subpopulation. Under these conditions, the focal subpopulation is well represented, whereas the neglected subpopulation goes unrepresented. More important, however, the population at large is as misrepresented as in (A).

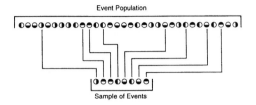

Event Population

Sample of Events

Random Exemplification
Model A

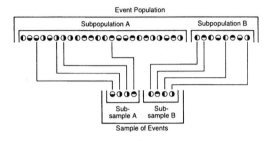

Event Population

Subpopulation A    Subpopulation B

Sub-     Sub-
sample A  sample B

Sample of Events

Stratified Exemplification
Model B

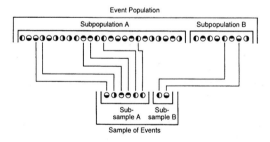

Event Population

Subpopulation A    Subpopulation B

Sub-     Sub-
sample A  sample B

Sample of Events

Proportional Exemplification
Model C

FIG. 1.2    Schemata of random exemplification. (A) From a finite population of events that vary along four attributes, a sample of events is randomly drawn. The population at large is represented without bias in that events of each attribute had the same chance for inclusion in the sample. If the events were carjackings (see legend to Fig. 1.1), all consequences for victims would be included approximately proportional with their occurrence, and an impartial, fair account of all carjackings would be provided. (B) Random samples are drawn from known subpopulations of the population of events. The samples are eventually combined to provide an unbiased representation. (C) Knowledge of the size of subpopulations is used to draw random subsamples that are proportional in size with that of their respective subpopulations. The combined subsamples provide an unbiased representation of the population of events. The procedural advantages of schemata (B) and (C) over schema (A) are described in the text. In terms of representational accuracy, these procedures may be treated as equivalent, however.

less drivers than that of women, or that the subpopulation of adolescents entails more than that of persons aged 30 to 50 years.

It should be emphasized that the exemplification procedures under consideration are *presentational* strategies. Which of these strategies will prove superior in terms of message reception, processing, retention, and retrieval is to be determined empirically. This is to say that presentational strategies may a priori offer impartial exemplification, but that information processing and its ultimate consequences, the perception of phenomena and the evaluation of issues, do not necessarily follow a priori considerations. How recipients interpret particular exemplifications, and how their interpretation affects their perception and judgment in the short and long term, is a posteriori and thus must be ascertained by empirical exploration. Such exploration constitutes, of course, the object of much of the exposition to follow.

### Exemplification of Unknown Event Populations

The exemplification of events of a population about which little, if anything, is known might be considered a misconception. Indeed, if the distribution of events in the population, especially in its subpopulations, is unknown, notions of representation, of impartial representation in particular, are inapplicable and misplaced. It would seem inappropriate, for instance, to consider two captured Indian headhunters from an entirely unknown tribe somewhere in the Amazon rain forest representative exemplars of all indigenous people of the region. Likewise, it would seem inappropriate to deem the articulated attitudes toward the institution of marriage by a handful of French youths representative exemplars of most, if not all, French adolescents.

Such inappropriateness does not preclude, however, that recipients of information about individual cases form impressions of a presumed population of similar cases. Recipients, as a rule, do nonconsciously infer that the properties observed in a few instances apply to the aggregate of like instances (Higgins, 1996; Lewicki, 1986; Nisbett, Krantz, Jepson, & Kunda, 1983). It is this deep-rooted inclination to generalize observed phenomena that gives individual events the status of exemplars.

Thus, although the representativeness of the exemplification of unknown populations is indiscernible from the perspective of presentational strategy, exemplification manifests itself post facto in the inference of an extended distribution of exemplified events. Alternatively expressed, the recipients' nonconscious inference of an extended distribution of events defines the events on which the inference is based as exemplars.

Although the representativeness of exemplification cannot be formally specified for unknown event distributions, inferences about population events are not entirely idiosyncratic on the recipients' part. Information conveyors using exemplars may invite or discourage inferences about presumed population events, thereby influencing the likelihood that recipients will arrive at either appropriate or unwarranted conclusions. They consequently have to assume some degree of responsibility for the presentation of exemplars, if the object is to provide an assessment of circumstances that is most likely to be correctly interpreted.

On intuitive grounds, then, the following guidelines may be suggested for the prevention of habitual misinterpretations of exemplars that are used under conditions where little or nothing is known about the event population.

1. As a premise, recipients are likely to interpret events not identified as unique or singular as exemplars of a larger event population. In other words, they tend to presume or infer by induction the existence of further similar events on the basis of a few known similar events. Figure 1.1 indicates this tendency to construct imagined populations essentially by the multiplication of observed exemplars.

2. Given this interpretational disposition, conveyors of information about unique, singular cases should specify that event status to prevent misinterpretation.

3. Information conveyors who provide exemplars without knowing the extent of their prevalence should indicate the lack of such knowledge in order to prevent misinterpretations.

It should be emphasized again that the effectiveness of these presentational strategies remains to be determined empirically. Specifically, it must be determined whether the reception, processing, retention, and retrieval of qualifying information, whose stimulus and ideational properties are likely to be less imposing than those associated with exemplifying happenings, can assert itself and function as a corrective, especially with the passage of time after exposure.

## EXEMPLIFICATION IN DIFFERENT DOMAINS OF COMMUNICATION

Exemplification permeates all domains of human communication. As our immediate experience with the events that constitute social and societal issues is limited, our perceptions and evaluations of, as well as our dispositions toward, these issues are largely formed on the basis of event accounts that others, who have observed or experienced the events under consideration, relate to us. Such event reports are, of course, communicated exemplars.

The original form of exemplar communication is, no doubt, the conveyance of others' direct observation or experience. Early hominids, for instance, may have learned from companions that certain mushrooms they ate prompted violent convulsions, whereas eating bone marrow made them feel great. The report of such experience by several companions should have invited the highly useful inference that the ingestion of the items in question will yield similar reactions in all others, oneself included.

Interpersonal exemplar communication is no less relevant in contemporary society. We still learn about the characteristics of specific populations or subpopulations from our friends and acquaintances. They might relate to us, for instance, that they got into a scuffle with hostile Punk fans or that they were bitten by geese. As a result, our dispositions toward members of these entity groups might shift toward greater caution. However, we might also learn from two coworkers in the office that some of their college-age daughters were divorced after less than a year of marriage and might be tempted to believe that early marriages do not last.

Communicated experience may not be truthful, of course, and impressions and dispositions formed on the basis of such revelations may be unreliable. This assessment applies especially to reports of exemplifying happenings that have not been directly experienced by the information conveyor, but by others who may have learned about the happenings from yet others. Potential distortions in such hearsay chains do not rule out, however, that the exemplars conveyed in them exert a degree of influence on the perception and judgment of issues involved.

In contemporary society, the conveyance of exemplars is largely delegated to professional organizations known as "the media." Newspapers, news broadcasts, and alternative, primarily electronic, computerized news delivery systems have made it their business to inform the citizenry about happenings and issues of concern from around the globe and beyond. We learn, for instance, of starvation in Somalia and are exposed to its exemplification: mostly the images of starved, gaunt children close to death (Sharkey, 1993). We similarly learn about Jews who call for the death of all Palestinians and about Palestinians who call for the death of all Jews (Gan, Hill, Pschernig, & Zillmann, 1996). Sometimes we learn how typical or atypical particular occurrences are. However, often it is left for the recipient to infer the frequency of occurrences of interest, the inference of prevalence and typicality being invited. In efforts of making a news story appear to address a relevant social issue, or on the mere suspicion that the exemplars might relate to a broader issue, reports conclude at times with assertions such as "This is by no means a single case!" or "We see this more and more!" (Brosius, Breinker, & Esser, 1991). On occasion, however, news reports can and do provide reliable information about the incidence rate of particular phenomena.

The latter is generally not the case for two obviously incompatible domains of exemplar communication: advertising and fiction.

Advertising, and public-relation efforts along with it, can be viewed as persuasive undertakings in which only supportive exemplars are selected. Nonsupportive and challenging exemplars are banned as counterproductive. For instance, in the form of personal testimonials exemplars abound in advertising. They consistently express satisfaction with, if not exuberance about, a product or service consumed. It is utterly unlikely that dissatisfaction is exemplified as part of a campaign. The same selectivity is found in the articulation of positive versus negative features of promoted products or services. This supportive–nonsupportive bias is reversed, of course, for competing products or services that are addressed in direct comparisons with promoted ones. Such comparisons appear to have become the rule in political advertising. It has been suggested, in fact, that political campaigns tend to give more emphasis to consistently negative exemplification of the intentions and actions of opponents than to the consistently positive exemplification of the intention and actions of the promoted candidates (Johnson-Cartee & Copeland, 1991). In short, advertising defines a domain of communication in which patently distorted exemplification is expected and accepted. Unlike news, the burden of exemplifying a population of happenings in impartial, representative fashion is not placed on advertising.

In this regard, and only in this regard, fiction parallels advertising. Fiction is obviously not tied to being veridical in its portrayals of the world. It is free to present happenings that have a high degree of similarity with persons, with creatures, with circumstances, and with events that actually exist or happened, respectively. Fiction is also free, however, to disregard totally any linkage to actual entities and events.

Granting that exemplifications in the fictional portrayal of entirely imagined worlds without resemblance to the realities before us (under the assumption that such fiction exists; cf. Ward, 1994) may not appreciably influence the judgment of earthly phenomena, fictional portrayals that claim a high degree of realism have been suspected of influencing the perception and evaluation of issues. For instance, it has been suggested that the abundance of fictional portrayals of interhuman killing fosters emotional callousness and promotes violence in adolescents eager to emulate their violent fictitious heroes (Geen & Thomas, 1986; Huesmann & Eron, 1986). Analogously, the focus on exemplars of victimization has prompted the contention that fiction consumers develop fears of becoming targets of violent crime themselves (Gerbner & Gross, 1976b; Gerbner, Gross, Morgan, & Signorielli, 1986). Moreover, it has been projected that the exemplification of sexual behavior in erotic fiction provides a distorted view of human sexuality and influences sexual dispositions and behaviors (Zillmann, 1989).

In the form of explicit pornography, erotica define a genre-admixture in combining elements of fiction with documentary, newslike elements. Such admixture is also found in historical portrayals of mostly political and cultural events. In the so-called *docudrama,* events that are purely fictional are intercut with events recorded in documentaries. Fictionalized reenactments are added to further confuse recipients about the fact–fiction status of event portrayals. It can only be suggested here that numerous fictional exemplars might be mistaken for exemplars from documentaries and from news programs, with the result that recipients process the information as veridical when they should not, thereby giving undue influence to fiction (Perry, Howard, & Zillmann, 1992).

Exemplification, finally, abounds in educational communication, including science education. The singular exemplar is typical. It is selected to serve as an analogue or an illustration of a principle. For instance, dropping objects of different weights from a tower in Pisa is a spectacular exemplar that helped Galileo to make an unforgettable point about gravity. So is the exemplar of Einstein's conception of gravity as an acceleration differential; that is, the exemplar that has us imagine the weight sensation of a person in an accelerating enclosure within an enclosure that is in free fall. Exemplars appear to have the capacity of making abstractions comprehensible—abstractions that are difficult to understand in their formal expression. Psychological phenomena, such as suspense, can be similarly exemplified. Hitchcock's (1959) account of a couple engrossed in a discussion while walking toward an open manhole on the sidewalk exemplifies all aspects critical to the experience of suspense: (a) protagonists in peril (i.e., in danger of knocking their teeth out), (b) their being oblivious to the danger, and (c) the audience being cognizant of it.

On the other hand, exemplification in education is no different from exemplification in other domains of communication in meeting with the same pitfalls when entity or event distributions associated with considerable uncontrolled variance are considered. Exemplars of typical murderers, typical sports fans, typical neurotics, typical Type A persons, typical feminists, and so forth, are likely to be rather nontypical in that they tend to be drawn from among the more extreme and memorable cases rather than from among the most frequently occurring ones.

# EXEMPLIFICATION
# IN PERSONAL EXPERIENCE

Personal experience can be viewed as the memory trace of continually encountered exemplars. Analogous to the chunking of information in communication, the flow of sensory information about external and, to a lesser degree, internal conditions is also broken down into manageable chunks. Pertinent circumstances and events are isolated and stored for later consideration. In other words, exemplars of immediately encountered conditions and events are aggregated in memory. The encounter of similar conditions and events is likely to activate this memory, adding to it as well. More important, whether consciously or unconsciously, this memory of exemplar experience is bound to influence related behaviors.

The conceptualization of experience as the result of the direct encounter of strings of exemplars obviously implies that individuals categorize happenings (Burns, 1992; Mervis & Rosch, 1981). Such categorization is implicit, in fact, in the adaptive behavior of all organisms capable of using retained information in their adjustment to changes in the environment (Griffin, 1984; Mackintosh, 1974; Pearce, 1994). For instance, brown rats are known to learn to avoid poisoned food by witnessing members of their pack ingest the food in question, exhibit convulsions, and die. They must be able, then, to causally connect specific food with ill effects and to store this exemplar experience for later behavior guidance. The indicated processes are the same, of course, for hominids who had to learn, for instance, the difference between becoming and unbecoming food items and between innocuous and dangerous animals.

The process by which we learn to associate properties with entities through the direct encounter with pertinent exemplars thus is a most fundamental one and does not depend on conscious information processing and elaboration (Bargh, 1984; Kissin, 1986; Lewicki, 1986). By direct encounter we learn, for instance, that it hurts to touch fire and to fall off a ladder, and that it does so consistently. On the other hand, we learn that not all dogs bite and that not all people are nice. We manage such cases in which covariation is less than perfect by acquiring a sense of the degree of consistency. If we encounter seven chow chows on different occasions, and they all turn out to be peaceful, we have an experiential basis for considering chow chows to be peaceful and, in future encounters, we will interact with them accordingly. Should they all turn out to be hostile, we form the opposite disposition and approach them henceforth with caution. Should two of them be friendly and the remaining five hostile, we are likely to be cautious but allow for exceptions. The point is that our dispositions reflect a quantitative assessment of exemplar experiences, not necessarily in precise numerical estimates but in proportional terms.

It should be recognized that the indicated ability served communication-deficient prehistoric humans rather well. As their expectations and dispositions were almost entirely based on personal observation of, and experience with, events of consequence, the exemplars encountered were likely to provide accurate, dependable information about the event group at large. Storage and retrieval of the covariation between pertinent phenomena and their attributes provided reliable behavior guidance in most vital situations. The possibility of encountering entirely atypical exemplars, such as gentle leopards or ferocious rabbits, existed of course, but the incidence of encounters of this kind can be considered to have been trivial and of little moment.

These circumstances changed drastically with the advent of representational communication. Expectations and dispositions now were subject to influence by others who related their observations and experiences, as well as by third parties who related their own observations and experiences to these others. Such extension of information about phenomena has, of course, enormous utility in making much personal experience superfluous and unnecessary. Perceptions and dispositions about a world of phenomena can be formed solely on others' observations and experiences. This potentially vast perceptual and dispositional enrichment comes at a risk, however. Its utility hinges on its veridicality, meaning the extent to which the conveyance of others' observation and experience is accurate and representative. The veridicality condition will not always be met, however, because the conveyed information may be modified and distorted to serve the conveyors' interests, intentionally or inadvertently so.

This assessment applies, of course, to communication in contemporary society. Specifically, it applies to all forms of interpersonal communication, to all levels of stratified communication, and to mass communication proper. Considering the news and also educational efforts, the available means of exemplar gathering entail the risk that the aggregation of exemplars in such expositions serves purposes other than the explicitly or implicitly declared provision of the highest degree of representativeness. Some distortions may serve ideological objectives, others the dictate of commercialism. Yet others may result from "established practice" and thoughtlessness. Whatever their cause, however, the problem of deficient representativeness of the exemplification of pertinent phenomena or issues by the communication media is inextricably linked to the preselection of exemplars intended to substitute for personal perception and experience.

## THE INTERFACE BETWEEN DIRECT
## AND MEDIATED EXPERIENCE

The substitution and expansion of personal perception and experience by the conveyance of others' perceptions and experiences raises the question as to whether mediated accounts of "reality" are treated as equivalent with direct observation and experience or are given lesser credence in the formation of judgments of phenomena and of dispositions toward issues. Moreover, the question arises as to whether presentational formats, such as news and fiction, exert similar or distinctly different degrees of influence on judgments and dispositions. Additionally, the mode of representation, iconic with high reproductive fidelity of audiovisual phenomena or symbolic with essentially no stimulus similarity between the message and its referent, may exert a degree of influence.

Using our chow chow illustration, would a neighbor's description of an attack by such a dog be as consequential as witnessing the attack? Would seeing the attack in the news or in a movie impact judgment similarly or differently? Might there exist a hierarchy of compellingness that starts with iconic representation in the news or documentary format, being followed by the symbolic representation in these formats, being followed in turn by fictional iconic portrayal, and ending with fictional symbolic representation? Or could it be that iconic representation, because of its sensory quality, generally dominates symbolic accounts, irrespective of the "reality status" ascribed by the format?

The possible interdependencies between format influence and personal experience have been addressed in the debate over the effects of media violence on crime apprehension. Violence in the media is prevalent in fiction, of course, but it is also featured in the news. Some investigators have lumped these formats together and, on the basis of their findings, have suggested a dominant influence of media portrayals of violence (Gerbner & Gross, 1976a). Others have challenged such contentions and have demonstrated that crime apprehension derives first and foremost from direct and quasi-direct experience with crime (Doob & Macdonald, 1979). Moreover, others have shown that violent crime reported in news/documentary format affects crime apprehension more strongly and for longer periods of time than does violent crime featured in fiction (Tamborini, Zillmann, & Bryant, 1984; Zillmann & Wakshlag, 1985).

Such discrepant findings leave the issue unresolved. However, this circumstance does not prevent many, who consider themselves media experts, to claim that fictional portrayals of violence are inconsequential for perceptions, dispositions, and behaviors related to violence. In endless debates of the issue, the asserted nil effect of fictional portrayals of violence and of other fictional or semifictional media fare, such as erotica, tends to be explained with the insinuation that "people know better." What is implied is that people readily identify the fiction format and, once they have accomplished that, are able to discard the information from consideration in the formation of judgments and dispositions concerning addressed real-life issues.

What appears to be common sense to many can be expressed in a tag model of presentational format. In such a model it is assumed that a format tag is stored along with exemplars; upon retrieval, the tag informs the individual that the associated information is either direct observation, mediated observation conveyed in news or documentary format, or mediated observation conveyed in fictional format. To the extent that the tag processing is conscious and deliberate, the indicated format segregation can be retained, and individuals would be afforded a degree of protection against undue media influence. The assumption of prolonged segregation of this sort is open to challenge, however. It can be argued that in an information-rich environment individuals are not able to trace exactly how they learned about particular accounts of events. They may be neither conscious of formats nor motivated to engage in efforts to protect themselves against influence associated with them — assuming that they could if they tried. As a result, they may confuse fact and fiction in many domains of perception and judgment.

Obviously, the issue can not be decided by purely conceptual examination. It remains to be determined empirically whether exemplars tagged "fiction" are without appreciable influence on judgments and dispositions, exemplars tagged "news" have some degree of influence, and exemplars tagged "experience" exert unwavering influence.

TWO

# Exemplification
# in Practice

· *American News*
  *News Magazines*
  *Television News*
  *Media Comparison*
· *Non-American News and Advertising*
  *Television-News Magazines*
  *Television Commercials*
  *Magazine Advertisements*
  *Comparison of Information Domains*
· *De Facto Exemplification in Fiction and in Quasi-Fiction*

This chapter provides a brief overview of the usage of exemplars in various media and information domains. The analysis focuses on the news, but it also addresses exemplification in other forms of media discourse, such as persuasion and entertainment.

## AMERICAN NEWS

In the media of the United States, exemplification abounds. Almost all news stories appearing in print feature exemplars. Television news involves exemplars less frequently, but it also presents them liberally. This is apparent from an analysis of U.S. media content that was conducted for the present volume by Gibson, Gan, Hill, Hoffman, and Seigler (1994).

### News Magazines

Reports in news magazines (*Newsweek, Time,* and *U.S. News & World Report*) have been examined in four arbitrarily drawn issues of 1994. The presence of exemplars, as well as their numbers, were coded for all reports. The length of stories and of exemplars was also recorded. Additionally, it was determined whether the featured exemplars were consistent with the discernible focus or "take" of a story, in disagreement with it, or neutral in this regard. Further assessments concerned such matters as the information source's relation to the reported issue (i.e., direct involvement, witness, or narration by a third party).

As Fig. 2.1 shows, 93% of all printed news stories featured exemplars. The use of three to four exemplars per story proved to be most characteristic (21% and 11%, respectively). The use of comparatively large sets of exemplars was also in evidence, however. In fact, one story not shown in the figure aggregated 40 case histories, and five others averaged 18.

On average, 9.12 exemplars were used per story. The average number of words serving the function of exemplification was 1,038. The average number of words of the stories themselves was 2,380. Thus, of the print-news stories that featured exemplars, a surprisingly large portion of text, about 44%, was dedicated to exemplification. The correlation between story length and accumulated exemplar length was $r = .62$, $p < .001$; that between story length and exemplar frequency was $r = .75$, $p < .001$. It stands to reason that stories grow with the amount of exemplification featured in them. In this connection it should be noted that print-news stories

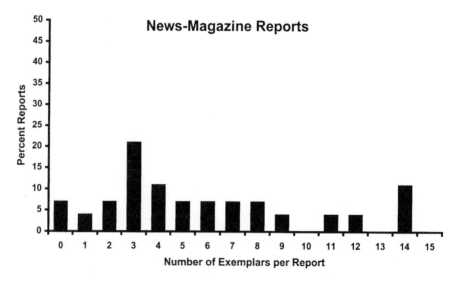

FIG. 2.1    Use of exemplars in news-magazine reports. The graph does not include the occasional excessive use of exemplars (e.g., 40 in one report; see text for details).

without exemplars had an average length of only 496 words. On average, then, stories featuring exemplars were nearly five times as long as stories devoid of exemplars.

Exemplification was mostly in line with the focus of the news reports (in 57% of all cases). In 25% of the cases, exemplars were inconsistent with that focus, thus constituting "exceptions to the rule" that potentially challenged the focal contention. In 18% of the cases, exemplars were coded as neutral (i.e., they had no discernible relevance to the story's stance). This yields a 70:30 percentage ratio for consistent, focus-supporting over inconsistent, focus-challenging exemplification.

The information source used to exemplify was directly involved with the addressed issue in about half of all cases (49%). Mere witnesses were rarely called on to give testimony (2%). In contrast, third-party narration was rather frequently employed (35%). In the remaining cases (14%), exemplification involved entities other than persons, usually concrete objects.

### Television News

Television-news reports were analogously examined. During May and June of 1994, five days, covering Monday through Friday, were randomly selected. On these days, the national news presented on the American networks ABC, CBS, CNN, and NBC were recorded. At a later time, the presence and frequency of exemplars were coded for all reports. The duration of reports (i.e., of the reports proper, without the anchor's introduction) and of their exemplars was measured as well. It was also determined whether the exemplars were consistent or inconsistent with the focus of the stories, or whether their content was not discernible as either consistent or inconsistent.

Figure 2.2 shows that television news often presents reports without exemplification. Almost half of all reports (47%) were devoid of exemplars. This circumstance may reflect the great pressure toward brevity that characterizes this medium. Consistent with such an interpretation is that exemplar-free reports were particularly short—45 seconds on average. This is in contrast to exemplified reports that averaged 139 seconds, their length thus exceeding that of exemplar-free reports by a factor of three. An alternative explanation of the rather high frequency of television-news reports without exemplification is, of course, this medium's so-called footage dependency; that is, the difficulty, and occasionally the impossibility, of attaining relevant audiovisual material fast enough for inclusion in a report may account for the high proportion of unexemplified reports.

On average, four exemplars were featured in those television-news reports that involved exemplars. The average accumulated time dedicated to story exemplification was 44 seconds, yielding an average exemplar duration of 11 seconds. Given the average report duration of 139 seconds, exemplification in television-news reports amounted to 32% or, roughly, one third. The correlation between report duration and the duration of exemplification was $r = .55$, $p < .001$; that between

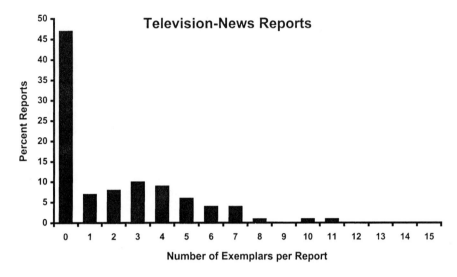

FIG. 2.2     Use of exemplars in television-news reports.

report duration and exemplar frequency was $r = .39$, $p < .001$. The length of exemplified reports obviously grows with the frequency and accumulated duration of the exemplars that they involve.

The contents of featured exemplars supported the reports' stance in 78% of all cases. In 10% of the cases, the exemplars were inconsistent with that stance. Exemplars were coded as neutral in 12% of the cases. The percentage ratio for consistent, focus-supporting over inconsistent, focus-challenging exemplification thus is 89:11.

### Media Comparison

In comparing exemplar usage in news-magazine reports with that in television-news reports, the strongest difference concerns the exemplar permeation of printed reports (93%). Only about half of the televised reports (53%) involved exemplars. The likely reasons for this discrepancy between these media under consideration have been indicated previously.

Regarding the number of exemplars used per report, the media share a modal usage: three exemplars. However, whereas for televised reports the use of similar frequencies diminishes steadily toward both lesser and larger numbers, the frequencies of exemplar use in printed reports are rather evenly distributed. The use of only a few exemplars (i.e., one or two) is similarly infrequent in both media. It is the use of large numbers of exemplars that separates them. Whereas televised reports are limited to small numbers (a maximum of 11 had been observed), printed reports may aggregate liberal amounts (as many as 40 had been observed).

As a result of these differences in the use of large numbers of exemplars, the correlation of frequencies across print and television is less pronounced than might be expected, $r = .69$, $p = .005$.

The exemplification volume (in terms of words for printed news and time for televised news) relative to report volume also differs appreciably. Perhaps reflecting the tendency to use larger sets of exemplars in printed reports, nearly half of the report volume (44%) was dedicated to exemplification in print news. In contrast, televised news dedicated only about one-third of the report volume (32%) to exemplars. Print news, then, relies more heavily on exemplification then does television news.

Substantial media differences are also apparent in the selection of exemplar content relative to the focus of news reports. Print news featured supportive versus challenging exemplars in a 7:3 ratio. Television news was appreciably more partial to supporting exemplars, featuring 89% of them. Only 11% of the exemplars challenged the report focus, yielding a supportive versus challenging exemplar ratio of approximately 9:1. To the extent that many or most issues are not one-sided, these ratios indicate that print-news reports tend to be more balanced in their involvement of exemplar content than are television-news reports. The greater partiality of television news to using supportive exemplification amounts to 19% (89% for television news as compared to 70% for magazine news) and again seems to reflect pressures toward brevity and limited exemplar numbers.

## NON-AMERICAN NEWS AND ADVERTISING

From outside the United States, detailed accounts of exemplar usage in the coverage of social, political, and economic issues by journalists are available for German media only. Daschmann and Brosius (1997) conducted an investigation of such usage in television-news magazines as well as in television and print advertising.

### Television-News Magazines

The investigation examined 27 reports in televised news magazines presented in five consecutive weeks in January and in February of 1995. The news magazines were aired by the public (ARD, ZDF) and commercial (RTL, SAT.1, PRO7, RTL2) German networks. Some were daily programs, whereas others were weekly programs. A total of 806 individual stories from 149 programs were analyzed. The presence of different types of exemplars and of different types of base-rate information was recorded. Of particular interest was whether or not the information provided in the exemplars was consistent with the base-rate information. It was also determined whether a news account addressed an isolated, singular event or a general phenomenon. In the latter case, the account is considered *generalizing* to the extent that it purports to apply to events above and beyond those about which information is provided—potentially to all events that constitute the phenomenon addressed in a report. In other words, observations on just a few events, on one event in the extreme, are generalized to similar but unobserved events. Claimed applicability, whether explicated or only implied, thus exceeds the realm of the limited account of incidents. Typical indicators of this kind of exemplification are statements like "This is only one of many instances . . . ," "It happens all the time . . . ," "This is by no means a single case . . . ," "It is more common than one might think. . . ." In this way, reporters suggest that their stories deal with issues composed of repeated and potentially frequent events of relevance, and they de facto claim that their account of a limited number of exemplars is representative of the general situation or defines a general trend. Whether or not base-rate information was provided was recorded only for such generalizing news accounts. The concreteness and the extent of documentation of base-rate information were also recorded. This entailed whether or not stories included quantification, cited independent sources and analyses, or presented tables or graphics. Also examined were the types of stylistic and rhetorical devices (i.e., event descriptions, interviews, inserted documents, etc.) as exemplars to support the report. In addition, story topics and the use of formal features were recorded.

*Topics.* The findings show news-story topics about evenly distributed across nine conventional content categories. Social issues (16%), human interest (15%), crime (14%), politics (13%), and culture (13%) were the leading ones. Because exemplification pertains to the generalization of information on limited numbers of events to information about a markedly larger aggregation of such events, further analysis concentrated on the stories featuring generalizing accounts. Accounts of this kind amounted to 59% of all stories. The percentage varied greatly, however, as a function of story topic. Concerning sports, only 25% of the stories contained generalization. In contrast, 83% of political stories entailed generalization. The difference reflects a focus on individuals versus general social phenomena. Reports about sports tended to center on individual athletes, teams, or contests without impetus to generalizing to similar persons or events. Coverage of political issues, on the other hand, almost always invited generalization.

*Types and Quality of Base-Rate Information.* In reports on general phenomena, it cannot be the isolated incident, or even a few arbitrarily aggregated incidents, that establish generality. It should not be surprising, therefore, that quantitative statements tend to be incorporated in generalizing reports. These statements, ranging from vague to precise, seem part and parcel of such reports. To ascertain the indicated variation, 474 generalizing stories were analyzed. Base-rate information was classified in terms of quantitative precision, validity, apparent intent, and visual format.

*Precision* refers to the presentation of specific quantities of occurrences under consideration (such as frequencies and ratios) versus the assertion of occurrence frequencies in roundabout fashion (such as "In many of these cases . . . ," "Most of the time . . . ," "In a minority of cases . . . ," ". . . almost never . . . ," or "It happens more and more frequently now."). *Validity* refers to the attribution of quantitative information to reliable sources (such as official statistics or surveys conducted by recognized agencies versus data from sources of unknown reliability, hearsay, or plain speculation). *Apparent intent* was manifest in generalizing claims made by anchors in lead-ins, in closing remarks, and during reports. *Visual format*, finally, refers to the presentation of quantitative information in graphics, in tables, or in charts.

*Precision.* In efforts to support the suggested generality of the reported phenomenon, precise quantities (i.e., frequencies, ratios, or rates of change) were provided only in a minority (44%) of the 474 stories. In the majority (56%) of stories, comparatively vague assertions, such as that the incidence "is skyrocketing," "has become commonplace," or "is increasing at an alarming rate," were made to insinuate a high rate of occurrence of focal events. Regarding the precision of reporting in these terms, marked differences were noted for the various topic areas. Stories on the economy, on accidents, on the environment, and on health issues offered the relatively greatest base-rate precision. Topic areas with low precision were human interest (15%), sports (20%), and cultural issues (24%). The discrepancy is readily explained by the greater availability of statistical information in the areas noted for superior base-rate precision.

*Validity.* Irrespective of the degree of precision of base-rate information, documentation of the source of the information may be expected. Journalistic standards require that claims of specific conditions be adequately researched and substantiated with appropriate data from official statistics, from commissioned surveys, from expert testimony, and the like. Specifying the sources of reported base-rate information would seem to be essential in giving recipients the means for judging the validity, or the lack thereof, of provided base rates. Surprisingly, only in 10% of the stories did the reporters adhere to the advisable journalistic practice of naming their sources. The large majority of stories, then, featured quantitative statements or displays without revealing the person or the agency responsible for the aggregation of this essentially statistical information. Failure to disclose the sources of base-rate information was observed for all topic areas.

These findings leave unclear whether generalizations are routinely made without adequate consideration of who supplies base-rate information (under which circumstances and with which potential partiality) or whether journalists are careless in naming sources, even omitting them on occasion in the interest of implied greater officiality. Either practice violates journalistic precepts of validation. Such violation has become apparent to the point where governmental agencies have registered complaints, in part perhaps because of the breaching of copyright laws (e.g., Statistisches Landesamt Baden-Württemberg, 1996).

A notable relation exists between validity and precision. Stories providing statistical data tended to indicate the sources of that information (22%). In contrast, stories without specific quantification almost always failed to reveal sources (1%). This relation suggests that journalists tend to cite specific base-rate information and its source when both are readily available, but that they tend not to name sources of imprecise quantification—possibly to give such information more credence than is warranted, as source revelation might prove the quantitative assertion tentative rather than being a reliable assessment.

*Apparent Intent.*    In the large majority of issue-projecting stories, generalization of the reported phenomenon occurred neither in the anchor's lead nor in his or her closing remarks, but during the story itself (87%). Generalizations during the anchor's lead or closing remarks were the exception. This was observed for all topic areas. Claims of the generality of a reported phenomenon thus came from within the reports themselves and not from anchors who introduce and interpret these reports.

*Visual Format.*    Base-rate information was almost never presented with visual aids, such as charts or tables. Almost all stories (87%) used spoken or written quasi-statistical statements without any kind of further visualization. Additional visual aids supporting base-rate information were used less frequently (in 13% of the stories). The use of visual aids differed, however, across topic areas. Reports on business (31%), environmental (25%), and health issues (27%) presented visually enhanced base-rate information with some regularity. In the remaining domains, however, such visual enhancement was comparatively rare (i.e., generally below 10%). An obvious relation between precision and visual format was obtrusively evident: tables and charts were linked to precise quantification.

The findings thus reveal that most of the reports in German television-news magazines are generalizing portrayals of phenomena. Base-rate information, if involved, is presented in the reports themselves rather than peripherally. Such information is mostly imprecise and rarely warrants the generalizations made. Moreover, base-rate information is mostly not attributed to sources. As a rule, it is presented verbally rather than visually.

*Exemplar Types and Stylistic Devices.*    The following two types of exemplars were distinguished in the analysis: The presentation of persons or events exhibiting or contradicting an asserted phenomenon (e.g., a story on the rise of pollution sickness incorporating verbal and pictorial information about the personal experience of patients who have recently suffered from pollution allergies) and interviews with witnesses of persons or events exhibiting or contradicting an asserted phenomenon (e.g., former patients or members of their families relating observations concerning pollution allergies). The distinction is essentially between *direct* and *indirect* exemplification.

Related stylistic devices were coded alongside the exemplars proper as follows.

1. Interviews with experts who confirmed or contradicted the phenomenon alleged or conveyed by the report (e.g., a physician asserting to treat increasing numbers of patients with pollution allergies).

2. Inserted documents confirming or contradicting the phenomenon alleged or conveyed by the report (e.g., releases from the governmental health department).

3. On-screen reporter appearances for the purpose of conveying official statements or expert opinions, mostly because of unavailability of pertinent film footage.

This classification of stylistic devices is by no means exhaustive. The three categories are, however, typical of television-news magazines. They are considered here in relation to the use of exemplars proper.

The indicated exemplars and stylistic devices were almost universally employed. They were absent from only 4 of the 474 stories (< 1%). At least one of the listed exemplars or devices was featured in more than 99% of the stories. Exemplars were observed in almost all stories (95%). Usage of stylistic devices was frequent as well (82%). It was observed, moreover, that one story in six (17%) worked exclusively with exemplars. In contrast, only 5% of the stories used stylistic devices exclusively.

Regarding the use of specific exemplar types and the stylistic devices, drastic differences were noted. Direct exemplars (i.e., the presentation of persons or events exhibiting or contradicting an asserted phenomenon) were used in almost all stories (92%). Indirect exemplars (i.e., the presentation of interviews with witnesses of persons or events exhibiting or contradicting an asserted phenomenon) were also frequently employed (76%). Stylistic devices were used more moderately. Expert interviews (57%) and inserted documents (55%) were presented in more than half of the cases. On-screen reporter appearances were markedly less frequently employed (in 15% of the stories). Considerable overlap was observed in the use of these devices (i.e., within stories, different devices were employed, and the use of particular ones was repeated).

The frequency of exemplar use is, of course, independent of purposeful, strategic exemplar usage. Exemplars may be employed to establish and enhance the significance of a phenomenon or the urgency of social issues. They may be used to further comprehension and appreciation of a situation. They also may be called on to persuade and incite action by stirring the emotions. All of these uses may serve an informational or persuasive objective. In order for exemplars to serve the indicated objectives, they must be consistent with them and invite generalization. However, exemplars may also be used to call the generality of a phenomenon into question. As explained earlier, they may be presented as exceptions to the rule. If they serve this function, they must be contradictory to, or at least inconsistent with, the primary objective of messages. From a journalistic perspective, the involvement of counterexemplars serves to document the existence of circumstances that oppose and challenge objective-serving generalizations that are based on the aggregation of consistent exemplars. If this presentation of counterexamples is supplemented by indications of the prevalence of such exceptions to the rule, the distribution of manifestations that are consistent or inconsistent of a phenomenon would be veridically described. In practice, however, such supplementary information seems rarely available and consequently tends not to be provided. In fact, counterexemplars, when their existence is acknowledged, are often dismissed as "exceptions." This practice amounts to a discounting of the potential significance of counterexemplars and gives normative status to exemplar-based generalizations. The use of claim-confirming and claim-contradicting exemplars was therefore examined. Exemplars that were neither confirmatory nor contradictory were coded as ambiguous.

Of the 3,425 exemplars that were classified, 96% confirmed generalizations. Disconfirming exemplars, then, are rarely employed. Practically all of the 448 stories containing exemplars used them as supportive evidence (99.6%). There were only two exceptions (.4%). Only in 9% of all stories were supportive exemplars complemented by contradictory ones.

The findings thus give strong evidence that in television-news magazines the aggregation of exemplars is exceedingly partial to supporting the primary contention of reports. Little, if any, attention is given to disconfirming and contradictory cases. Moreover, the prevalence of these cases is left unspecified and often, by explicit insinuation or implicitly, is characterized as trivial (e.g., disconfirming cases are declared exceptions, which suggests scarcity and atypicality). The extreme one-sidedness of issue exemplification in television-news magazines is most apparent in the percentage ratio of 96:4 for the usage of story-stance-supporting over challenging exemplars.

### Television Commercials

Compared to news, as well as to alternative informational presentations and entertainment programming, commercials serve a different, unique purpose and tend to be differently formatted. Commercials are designed to persuade viewers to purchase certain products or services. They are, as a rule, restricted to a very short presentation time (i.e., the majority of commercials in Germany as well as in many other countries being limited to a duration of about 30 seconds). Assuming that exemplars are effective persuasion devices, their frequent and—owing to their persuasive mission—one-sided use in commercials should be expected. The time restriction sets limits, however, for the aggregation of exemplars.

Exemplification was analyzed in a sample of German television commercials. The commercials were taken from eight channels (ARD, ZDF, RTL, SAT.1, PRO7, RTL2, Kabel1, and VOX) in October of 1996 and in February of 1997. Three types of exemplars were distinguished. *Presentation* exemplars were those that demonstrated the use of particular products or services by individuals or groups to the apparent satisfaction of the users (e.g., a toothpaste commercial showing one or several persons before, during, and after product use, along with the promised effect of these persons' healthy, white teeth). *Endorsement* exemplars were testimonials by one or by several persons, often celebrities, who acknowledged positive experience with particular products and services (e.g., well-known athletes attributing their success, at least in part, to special clubs or rackets). On occasion, these testimonials included explicit appeals for using the products and services in question. *Demonstration* exemplars, finally, were those that focused on properties of products and services rather than on their users. Often in comparison to competing products and services, advantages of the advertised items were shown and articulated (e.g., a detergent being shown, usually by sales personnel, yielding superior results while costing less).

A total of 1,733 commercials were analyzed. Presentation exemplars amounted to 34% of the 583 commercials. Thus, in about one third of the commercials one or more users were shown being satisfied with, if not clearly happy and ecstatic about, the consumption experience. This type of exemplar featured "common people" (i.e., unknown men and women from all walks of life) with great regularity (84%). Endorsement exemplars were less frequent with 182 (11%) of all cases. In 10% of these exemplars, recommendations were made by celebrities. In another 10%, endorsements came from persons presented as experts. Demonstration exemplars, with 590 cases (34%), were as frequent as presentation exemplars. Focusing on commercials, in about 71% of them at least one of the three types of exemplars was used. Employment of more than one exemplar type within commercials was observed in 8% of the cases.

Taken together, it is apparent that television advertising is permeated with exemplars and that advertisers must believe them to be potent persuasive devices. It is also important to note that exemplification, as expected, is totally partial to the portrayal of promoted products and services in the most positive terms possible. Such portrayal denies the involvement of exemplars that would challenge asserted qualities of promoted entities. It should not be surprising, therefore, that television advertising is entirely devoid of counterexemplars.

## Magazine Advertisements

Compared to television commercials, the capacity for exemplification seems even more restricted. Information presentation is essentially reduced to one frame. Exemplar use nonetheless typifies print advertising. This was established by the analysis of advertisements in three popular German magazines (*Stern, Focus,* and *Bunte*) published in three consecutive issues in April of 1997. The exemplar types described for television commercials were used.

The nine analyzed issues contained 521 advertisements. Of these, 71 (14%) contained presentation exemplars. Endorsement exemplars were most frequent with

128 cases (25%). Demonstration exemplars were observed in 82 cases (16%). Compared to television commercials, then, presentation and demonstration exemplars were used less frequently, whereas endorsement exemplars were used more frequently. The print advertisements also differed from television commercials in terms of endorsement and demonstration personnel. In print, 80% of the exemplars featured celebrities, in contrast to only 3% in commercials. In 48% of the cases, celebrities demonstrated products, and in 18% they explicitly recommended them. Overall, 55% of the ads involved one of the three exemplar types, compared to 80% of the television commercials. However, as was the case with commercials, print advertisements were entirely partial to presenting claim-supporting exemplars. Counterexemplification, as expected, was not in evidence.

## Comparison of Information Domains

The data provided by the investigations of Gibson, Gan, Hill, Hoffman, and Seigler (1994) and Daschmann and Brosius (1997) do not allow an international comparison because different types of news presentation were examined (i.e., American national television news and German television-news magazines). However, under the assumption that presentational formats do not appreciably differ between American and German programs, a tentative comparison of these formats, including print presentations of news and commercial persuasive formats, may be offered.

Table 2.1 summarizes the comparison. As can be seen, reports in television-news magazines and in print-news magazines show the highest degree of exemplar permeation. Conventional daily news reports appear to feature significantly fewer exemplars. At least a partial reason for this may be the severe restriction of preparation time for these reports. Television advertising shows a high degree of exemplar permeation. In contrast, and presumably a result of the limited presentational capacity of the one-page ad, the exemplar permeation is moderate in print-magazine advertisements.

TABLE 2.1
Exemplar Permeation of Informational and Persuasive Presentations
and the Distribution of Exemplars Consistent and Inconsistent
With Generalizing Assertions and Proposals

| Communication Domain | Exemplar Permeation (% Per Presentation) | Exemplar Distribution (% Consistent : Inconsistent) |
|---|---|---|
| News | | |
| Television reports | 53 | 89:11 |
| Television magazines | 95 | 96:04 |
| Print magazines | 93 | 70:30 |
| Advertisements | | |
| Television commercials | 80 | 100:00 |
| Print-magazines ads | 55 | 100:00 |

More revealing, perhaps, is the ratio of exemplars that support the stance of reports versus exemplars that challenge it—or that at least qualify its universality. Advertising obviously constitutes an extreme in that it generally fails to acknowledge claim-diminishing conditions. Television-news magazines, however, exhibit similarly extreme partiality in the aggregation of supportive exemplars. Daily television-news reports approximate this imbalance in exemplifying a general phenomenon. Print-magazine news, probably because of comparatively little time pressure on the compilation of pertinent information and also because of its relative image independence, shows the best balance in the display of stance-supporting exemplars and in the exemplification of alternative manifestations of the phenomenon under consideration.

The use of exemplars in educational and in scientific discourse has not been systematically investigated at this point, and reliable comparisons, hence, are not possible. However, it would seem reasonable to assume that the pursuit of educational objectives will also entail partiality in the aggregation of supportive exemplars. Educational discourse, much like news-magazine discourse that has an educational mission, is unlikely to present exemplar distributions in accordance with their relative incidence rate. The presentation of scientific explorations and accomplishments in textbooks and in television programs is similarly mission-bound. Perusal of such exposition has shown that exemplars tend to be particularly partial to supporting the discussed phenomena, as illustrations are to exhibit "typical" occurrences in memorable fashion—which usually demands the sacrifice of the not-so-typical occurrences. Be this as it may, the systematic comparison of these discourse forms with news and advertising formats requires, and thus must await, less informal assessments of the exemplifications they manifest.

## DE FACTO EXEMPLIFICATION
## IN FICTION AND IN QUASI-FICTION

Since Berelson and Salter's (1946) early demonstration of bias in the representation of majority and minority Americans in magazine fiction, representation by fictional exemplification has attracted much attention by communication scholars.

By way of content analysis, Berelson and Salter (1946) determined the proportions of ethnic groups, such as Blacks and Jews, featured in protagonist roles and related these proportions to those of the groups in the general population. Gross underrepresentation was observed, along with its mirror image of gross overrepresentation of Whites in leading roles.

Gerbner and his collaborators (e.g., Gerbner, Gross, Morgan, & Signorielli, 1986) have applied this technique to prime-time television and have recorded a host of misrepresentations. For instance, compared with women in the cast of fictional characters, men were found to be overexemplified by a factor of three. Teens and the elderly were found to be grossly underexemplified. The exemplification of minorities was found to be similarly nonrepresentative, with Blacks reaching only three fourths and Hispanic Americans one third of their presence in the population. Regarding the overrepresentation of crime and its curtailment in fiction, the law enforcement personnel alone outnumbered all blue-collar and service workers by a far margin.

Greenberg, Simmons, Hogan, and Atkin (1980) similarly assessed fictional television characters by a set of their features and then compared the characters' prevalence to census data. These investigators reported an underrepresentation of women, children, older people, craftsmen, and clericals, as well as an overrepresentation of persons aged 20 to 50 and managers. In contrast, and irrespective of particular roles, the relative frequencies of Black and White characters were found to be fairly representative.

Exemplifications, however, cannot always be matched against known distributions of entities in defined populations. Analyses often serve to establish exemplification trends or to compare the exemplifications in various domains of communication. Seggar (1977), for instance, examined short-term trends (1971–1975) in the portrayal of minorities and women. The findings show gains by women and by Blacks, but losses by other minorities. Such observations may serve as checks on the effectiveness of representational policies or can be used in defining these policies.

Dominick (1973) ascertained the exemplification of crime on prime time television and documented the medium's gross partiality to murder and assault. Zillmann and Weaver (1997) focused on crime in the movies instead. They compared violent action in recent blockbuster movies with that in less recent films and found that the number of violent episodes in the recent movies doubled. The time dedicated to displaying these episodes grew alongside this increase by 50%. The exemplification of violent death grew tenfold for protagonists and ninefold for antagonists. Sadistic killings emerged as a novel type of exemplar. Sapolsky and Molitor (1996) reported similar trends for violence in horror movies.

Exemplification has also been ascertained, however, for genres devoid of the display of grievous asocial behaviors. It has been shown, for example, that intergender put-downs in prime-time comedy are at a par (Stocking, Sapolsky, & Zillmann, 1977). Men were as much the butt of jokes delivered by women as women were of jokes delivered by men. Men participated three times as often as women in comic exchanges, however. Men thus enjoyed far more "air time."

Even more removed from significant social implications are things such as the exemplification of the ethnicity and the gender of lead performers of popular music on different music-television channels. Brown and Campbell (1986), for instance, reported a preponderance of White male stars on MTV (83%). Black male stars dominated Video Soul instead (54%). The same channel partiality was evident for minority female stars (11% and 19%, respectively).

The exemplification of sexual behaviors has also undergone extensive exploration (e.g., Brown & Bryant, 1989; Palys, 1986). Brosius, Weaver, and Staab (1993), for instance, showed that in pornographic films the exhibition of female dominance over males had tripled in a decade's time. During the same period, the initiation of sexual activities immediately on the encounter of strangers doubled.

Suffice it here to point out that exemplification outside the news context has been a matter of concern. The deliberate or inadvertent misrepresentation of social reality by misexemplification in fiction and in quasi-fiction (such as in pornography) is apparently thought capable of fostering misperceptions and misjudgments. We return to this issue in chapter 4 and provide evidence indicating that these effect expectations are not unfounded.

# THREE

# Information
# Processing

· *The Function of Schemata*
· *Heuristics and Their Influence*
    *The Representativeness Heuristic*
    *The Availability Heuristic*
    *Vividness and Salience*
    *Chronic Accessibility*
· *Emotion as a Mediator*
    *Empathic and Counterempathic Reactivity*
    *Differently Diminishing Accessibilities*
· *Contingency Processing*
    *The Informative Function*
    *Affect Enhancement*
    *Model–Observer Affinity*

I nformation processing, as a paradigm (cf. Broadbent, 1958), has played and is playing a decisive role in cognitive psychology. According to this approach, cognition is a sequence of individual processing stages. The sequence begins with a stimulus being translated into a perception pattern by physiological processes. If a section of this pattern attracts attention, a block of working memory is allocated to it. Rehearsal and elaboration processes subsequently serve to transfer some of the original stimulation into long-term memory stores. During recall, these stores are searched, and bits of information are retrieved and placed at the disposal of working memory. Models presented by Atkinson and Shiffrin (1968) and Waugh and Norman (1965) entail and integrate the various indicated basal processes.

Psychologists have been able to use these simple information-processing models to explain elementary cognitive operations (e.g., the retention of word lists). It was not possible, however, to explain the more complex cognitive processes, such as the comprehension of circumstances and their interrelations. The principal deficiency of the early information-processing models was the implicit assumption that information is processed, as a rule, by rather inactive, indifferent, and unprepared individuals. This supposition proved untenable (cf. Anderson, 1980; Eysenck & Keane, 1990).

Research has shown that the processing of information is greatly affected by a host of conditions prevailing at the time. Past experiences, dispositions deriving from them, and numerous situation-determined factors have been found to exert a considerable degree of influence on such processing. As a result, more recent theories have concentrated on and emphasized an interaction between stimulus-driven and concept-driven processing. Stimulus-driven (or "bottom-up") processing signifies that processing is steered mainly by the external stimulus environment. Concept-driven (or "top-down") processing, in contrast, signifies that processing is guided primarily by expectations based on past experience (Bransford, Barclay, & Franks, 1972; H. H. Clark & Clark, 1977; Danks & Glucksberg, 1980). Top-down processing occurs, for instance, when ambivalent figures or words are interpreted in accord with past experience. Bottom-up processing is evident in the control of attention by potent environmental stimuli. As a rule, however, bottom-up and top-down information processing occur jointly and simultaneously (Navon, 1977; Neisser, 1976). Perceptual operations, then, entail the filtering of direct percepts through a system of experience-based expectations (Bruner, 1951, 1957; Postman, 1951; Stark & Ellis, 1981).

## THE FUNCTION OF SCHEMATA

Psychologists have identified semantic memory, or semantic structures in memory, as the cognitive structures that are responsible for expectation- or hypothesis-controlled perception (Anderson & Bower, 1973; Kintsch, 1974; Tulving, 1972). Such cognitive structures have been conceptualized as *schemata* that influence the processing of perceptual input. The schema concept, first introduced by Bartlett (1932) and by Piaget (1928), has been widely adopted in the social sciences (Axelrod, 1973; Brosius, 1991).

A *schema* is an active structure in memory that connects existing assumptions about how the external world is to be seen and dealt with, as well as how objects, events, and persons are to be classified. The premise of all schema-based approaches is that, as perceptual and memory-related processes modify and thus prevent the sheer mechanical storage of percepts, recipients actively construct a representation of the environment around them. This way of thinking is reflected in the uses and gratifications approach to media influence (Palmgreen, Wenner, &

Rayburn, 1980; Rubin & Perse, 1987) and in transactional effect models of communication generally (Früh & Schönbach, 1982). The focus on the recipient does not mean, however, that schema-based theories neglect the role of the stimulus environment. Schemata are thought to be acquired over time in the confrontation with large numbers of basal stimuli. The formed schemata then give structure to eclectic impressions, and they, in turn, are modified and refined by these impressions. Schema conceptualizations take into account that only a fraction of the encountered information is taken in and processed. Central to such reasoning are criteria for information selection and processing that enable persons to concentrate, in a relatively quick and efficient manner, on personally useful aspects of the incoming information flood.

Schemata are thought to guide the interpretation and classification of perceptions of persons, of objects, and of events in the environment. Their operation is considered an automatic process that eludes the recipients' conscious control. The acquisition and use of schemata can be attributed to a basic human ability to identify common attributes of all conceivable entities (Anderson, 1980). Once in place, schemata are thought to guide the interpretation of structurally similar entities, regardless of their individual peculiarities. The indicated classification or categorization follows specific sets of identified attributes.

Schema conceptualizations do not claim universal applicability, however. Not all encountered stimuli are seen as being filtered through schemata. Some objects and events may not relate to existing schemata. Tulving (1972, 1983) distinguished between episodic and semantic memory to accommodate this situation. It is suggested that in early developmental stages the perception of reality is made up of separate perceptual episodes that are stored in an unintegrated fashion. Episodes can be understood as impressions of surroundings limited in time and in space. Owing to the discussed ability to identify common attributes and to classify these episodic impressions, they are eventually converted to semantic memory, along with the conversion schemata. This transformation of a multitude of episodes into a small number of semantic structures can be seen as a process that fosters efficiency of processing and economy of thought in dealing with complex environments.

It is generally assumed that, concerning the reception of media presentations, schematic information processing dominates episodic processing. The reason given for this dominance is the uniformity of abundant precepts. Mass-media displays especially are seen as being repetitive and stereotypical. Television news, in particular, has been said to present its largely repetitive contents in cyclical fashion (Ballstaedt, 1977; Ballstaedt & Esche, 1976; Dahlgren, 1983; Winterhoff-Spurk, 1983). Regarding reception, it is suggested that viewers have acquired news schemata that lead to a channeling or filtering of presented information. Limited storage and processing capacity, relative to the enormity of simultaneously available information, is again invoked as an argument for the need, if not the necessity, of processing information within established schemata.

The most extensive application of schema theory to the reception of mass-media content concerns news programs. Graber (1984) posited that schemata serve at least four different functions in news processing. First, they determine which information will be absorbed for further processing. As a consequence, this step also determines which information is available for recall at later times. Second, schemata assist the classification of novel information and integrate it into existing perceptions, evaluations, and dispositions. Third, they enable recipients to refine related schemata by fostering inferences that close gaps in schema-defined knowledge. Finally, schemata aid in solving problems by supplying likely scenarios and potential solutions. Graber (1984) contends that without schemata people would not be able to sensibly reduce the vast amount of incoming information and to extract essential meaning from it. According to Graber (1984), schematic processing is the principal reason for the fact that recipients quickly forget the specifics and the details of news reports and retain only roundabout impressions and global interpretations (cf. Gunter, 1987). As whatever is retained becomes subject to highly personal schematic filtering, Graber's (1984) vision (see also Winterhoff-Spurk, 1983) readily extends to the view that the news, because it offers little that is truly novel, does not demand adjustments of well-defined schemata. Such a view renders the news an orienting message system that is unlikely to critically alter the citizens' established perceptions of public affairs.

In an essentially qualitative study, Graber (1984) conducted extensive interviews that established a firm connection between individuals' past experience and their apparent usage of particular schemata. She consequently concluded that the most helpful feature of schema theory is its capacity to explain why people are able to extract personally relevant information out of the flood of information transmitted by the mass media.

In numerous investigations, the information extracted from news programs was found to be less specific than the investigators had expected (Gunter, 1987). Given such disconfirmation of expectations, Graber (1984) suggested that the findings of studies that focused on the retention of details and secondary particulars created the erroneous impression of poor information transfer from media presentation to recipient. She insisted that there exists rather effective extraction of personally salient but potentially esoteric information. The esoteric component of the extraction would seem to signal a risk accruing to schematic processing. To the extent that this kind of processing is controlled by highly varying individual past experience, information extraction will vary greatly along with it, and communally significant information may go unrecognized, unprocessed, and unabsorbed.

It would seem fair to say that media-effect conceptualizations have failed to produce a well-elaborated schema theory on the basis of which specific influences could be anticipated and accurately predicted. The schema construct is marred by considerable conceptual imprecision, and this has led to vagueness and ambiguities in effect projections (Brosius, 1991). It can be said, in fact, that schema conceptualizations are not so much serving effect predictions as they are giving a degree of plausibility to post facto accounts of observed media effects. This notwithstanding, the proposal that information processing is greatly influenced by the recipients' past experiences, dispositions, and habits can be considered generally accepted among effects researchers and communication scholars (Woodall, 1986).

Many issues remain unresolved, however. Except for Graber's (1984) pertinent demonstrations, the degree of involvement and influence of schema processing in news reception has not been explored. For media genres other than the news, schema processing has gone entirely unexplored. Moreover, it has remained unresolved whether the employment of schemata is universal or is reserved for confrontations with phenomena characterized by high stimulus complexity. The extent to which schemata are linked to certain types of content or function as formal decision algorithms has remained unclear as well. It is often assumed that schemata are hierarchically organized from low to high levels of abstraction (e.g., Sherman, Judd, & Park, 1989; Taylor & Crocker, 1981), but the conceptualization and operationalization of the presumed abstraction levels also has remained controversial.

Despite its somewhat hazy contours, the schema concept is not without merit in the consideration of the influence of media content. There can be no doubt that, in the organism's confrontation with the complexity of environmental stimulation prevailing at any given time, the information onslaught is subjected to filtering that takes out whatever is not immediately relevant. Relevance, definable as a quality that acknowledges the utility of judged entities, is of course subjectively defined. The conceptualization of such personalizing selectivity by means of constructed schemata offers an avenue for coming to terms with the issue of information reduction during processing. Recipients of media messages may therefore be seen as constructing their own information units and configuring phenomena in their own way. More than a century ago now, William James (1890) expressed this view in succinct fashion:

> Millions of items of the outward order are present to my senses which never properly enter into my experience. Why? Because they have no *interest* for me. . . . Only those items which I *notice* shape my mind—without selective interest, experience is an utter chaos. Interest alone gives accent and emphasis, light and shade, background and foreground—intelligible perspective, in a word. (p. 402)

Claims of a lack of isomorphism between the information units in media presentations and those in the heads of the recipients thus amount to no more than an acknowledgment of variance in utility filtering. It must be recognized, however, that this variance is limited, and that a considerable degree of commonality may exist between phenomena presented in the media and these phenomena reported by the recipients of the presentations in question. Numerous investigations of perceptions formed on the basis of news reports, for instance, demonstrate convincingly that a high degree of correspondence is the rule (Brosius & Staab, 1989; Brosius, Staab, & Gaßner, 1991; Kepplinger, 1989; McCombs, 1994), this despite the indicated subjectification by schematic processing. Such commonality in information selectivity and filtering does not elude schema conceptualizations, but it has been underestimated and neglected in schema theorizing. It would seem imperative for schema theories, if they are to provide a more complete elucidation of the processes that arbitrate perceptions and dispositions by way of intake of media presentations, to accept the interindividual commonality of a multitude of schemata in addition to personalized ones, as well as the joint operation of all these schemata.

## HEURISTICS AND THEIR INFLUENCE

The limited processing capacity of the human brain is of central importance in an alternative psychological approach to information processing. *Heuristics,* conceivable as mechanisms that simplify and expedite information intake and utilization, are the essentials of this approach.

Evaluations and judgments of issues, of social issues in particular, are often made without apparent elaboration. It appears that people usually can not, or simply do not, take the time to sift through all known facets of an issue, ponder their relative importance, and then derive a careful appraisal. The "streamlining" of processing, and ultimately of rendering judgment, is obviously economical in the sense of reducing processing effort and time. The use of heuristics thus serves efficiency and expediency of thought. Such convenience and proficiency comes at a cost, however. It should be appreciated intuitively that heuristic processing, as it simplifies and cuts corners, entails a risk of erroneous judgment that tends to exceed that associated with deliberate, careful contemplation. Numerous psychological investigations have demonstrated the judgmental errors that are invited by heuristic processing or that are its inevitable result (Fiske & Taylor, 1984; Higgins & Bargh, 1987; Kahneman, Slovic, & Tversky, 1982; Sherman et al., 1989; Tedeschi, Lindskold, & Rosenfeld, 1985).

Heuristic information processing, and the judgmental errors associated with it, applies to common social discourse. Media communication is not exempt. In fact, it can be argued that the judgmental error risk of heuristic processing is particularly high for the reception of mass-media presentations. This is because the media context limits the recipients' ability to attain corroborating or contradictory information. Recipients are, so to speak, at the mercy of information providers. As they are deprived of means to verify or falsify, selective and necessarily incomplete accounts of phenomena—whether impartial or deliberately or unintentionally distorted— are likely to be accepted as veridical. Regarding news reports, for instance, recipients are limited to the bits and pieces of information that journalists have preselected and preinterpreted for them. Recipients, then, are at a loss when absorbing the news. They could not, even if they wanted to, conduct elaborative assessments. The use of less than exhaustive evaluative procedures, such as heuristics, is thus literally forced on them. However, the use of convenient judgmental procedures is also invited by the fact that much news content is not especially important to recipients, and getting a general impression is seen as sufficient by them. In other words, recipients may be unwilling to invest great processing efforts into elaborative assessments of nonsalient issues and may readily resort to heuristic processing. Finally, the sheer amount of information presented in the news and elsewhere in the media can be seen as fostering a preference for convenient, expedient processing.

Theorizing in terms of heuristic information processing entails the central assumption that people perceive their world, especially their social environment, not exactly as should be expected on the basis of accepted standards of formal reasoning and quasi-scientific interpretation (Hastie, 1983; Higgins & Bargh, 1987; Showers & Cantor, 1985). Needs, values, and expectations are thought to influence the perception and interpretation of relevant entities and happenings. People confronted with social issues do not, as a rule, examine them by carefully gathering and weighing all available or conceivable relevant information—as detached beings of high rationality might. This premise is long-standing (Heider, 1958; Mischel, 1968) and permeates a vast number of psychological investigations that explore judgmental process (Landman & Manis, 1983; Markus & Zajonc, 1985; Ostrom, 1984; Sypher & Higgins, 1988). The purpose of the present discussion is not, however, to provide an exhaustive overview of the indicated extensive literature. Rather, it is to elucidate the theoretical basis of various pertinent concepts with a small number of selected pivotal investigations, especially investigations that have clear implications for the reception and interpretation of news reports.

It is a common belief about the effects of the media that featured reports can have stronger or weaker influence, depending on exactly how they are presented. Respondents' attention may be engaged by imaginative plays on words or by extraordinary photographs; as a result, respondents may recall their impressions for extended periods of time and potentially be influenced by them. A single picture of sludge spewing from a sewer pipe into a river, for instance, might influence perceptions and judgments of pollution more than detailed accounts of the number and amount of pollutants in the river. Such assessments are obviously less than judicious and are bound to be erroneous, irrespective of the particular degree of their presumed prevalence.

Tversky and Kahneman (1971, 1973, 1974, 1982; Kahneman & Tversky, 1972) examined how informational displays are processed and how judgments are formed on the basis of such processing. They identified the existence of various heuristic mechanisms that are used to render speedy decisions in the face of complex and uncertain situations. These heuristics can be construed as rules of thumb that help reduce the time needed to process incoming information. By using such shortcut procedures, the multitude of appraisals and decisions that need to be made more or less continually can be performed quasi-automatically and in routine fashion. Heuristics are, for the most part, generalizations that are based on limited individual experience, a circumstance that makes them especially prone to distortion. Two heuristics are of particular importance in this context.

### The Representativeness Heuristic

Many everyday decisions require assessing the likelihood that a certain object or person belongs to a certain class of objects or persons. In the case of news reception, for instance, problems in need of resolution may be expressed as questions like "Does politician X belong to the group of hyperliberals?" Recipients routinely use the *representativeness heuristic* to answer such questions. In principle, a specific case is classified as belonging to a class of cases if the attributes of the case are similar to the attributes of the class.

Kahneman and Tversky (1973) examined the "error of judgment" that occurred in these inferences. They worked with personality descriptions in their research. Respondents were shown profession-specific descriptions of persons and were told that these persons were arbitrarily selected lawyers and engineers. In one condition, the respondents were informed that 70% of the descriptions were of lawyers; in the other condition, only 30% were said to be those of lawyers. Eventually, the respondents were asked whether they thought specific persons were lawyers or engineers. In both test conditions, the respondents estimated that 50% of the personalities described were lawyers, reflecting their actual, random distribution. Their judgments were based solely on the described attributes and were not influenced by the percentages, although these were explicitly stated.

Tversky and Kahneman (1982) specified the operation of the representativeness heuristic as follows.

1. People do not base their decision on stated probabilities, but rather on the attributes of the specific case, which they then extend to all cases. This phenomenon was termed the *base-rate fallacy* (Bar-Hillel, 1980; see also Gavanski & Roskos-Ewoldsen, 1991; Ginosar & Trope, 1987; Good, 1968; Huff, 1959; Meehl & Rosen, 1955; Tversky & Kahneman, 1980).

2. People do not take different sample sizes into consideration when making a decision. Although inferences drawn from small samples are not nearly as reliable as those drawn from larger ones, respondents draw essentially the same conclusions from these samples (Kahneman & Tversky, 1972). This misjudgment applies even to persons with considerable statistical knowledge. It has been demonstrated, for instance, that students with basic training in statistical inference could be easily misled in contexts where the law of large numbers applies (Schaller, 1992).

3. People misconceive the role of chance. If respondents were asked which combination of lottery numbers was more likely to be drawn, either the series 1–2–3–4–5–6 or the series 4–12–23–24–37–45, most chose the second series because it resembled lottery draws they were used to seeing. The chance of drawing either series is the same, of course.

Tversky (1977) thought that the representativeness heuristic entailed matching processes. An object's similarity to a class of objects stored in memory must be discerned on the basis of a series of attributes. Individuals essentially determine the degree of correspondence between the object being judged and the stored attributes. If this degree is sufficiently high, the matched object is deemed a member of the class.

The work of Tversky and Kahneman (e.g., 1971, 1973, 1974) spawned numerous related investigations, some of which involved information processing comparable to that in situations of media communication. Hamill, Wilson, and Nisbett (1980), for instance, provided respondents with brief descriptions of welfare recipients and of prison inmates (case histories or exemplars). The descriptions were said to be characteristic or uncharacteristic for the overall population of welfare recipients or of prison inmates. In addition, the respondents were given information about the overall population of welfare recipients or of prison inmates (i.e., statistics on race, religion, etc.) The findings revealed that the respondents ignored the labels (characteristic vs. uncharacteristic) when making judgments. Their decisions were based on the observed characteristics of each particular case and were not influenced by the more valid statistical information.

In other words, although the specifications in the case histories were not as reliable as the statistical information provided about the overall population of welfare recipients, the concrete cases still had a greater influence on judgment. This interpretation also can be found in prototype research (cf. Rosch, 1973, 1975, 1977). Different concepts are thought to be connected to a prototype that most closely corresponds with considered concepts. If an object being judged is similar to the prototype, all attributes of the prototype will be ascribed to the object, even if all details do not apply in the specific case.

Applying these rationales and findings to news reception, the inevitable conclusion is that recipients will neither consider all aggregated facts nor evaluate them in a consistent manner when assessing situations. As a rule, information is not being evaluated in a detached, objective, and sciencelike fashion. Rather, information is processed in a simplified form and is strongly filtered through personal systems of experience-based categorization. Statistical information and stated probabilities tend to have less influence on judgment than do concrete case histories because, concerning everyday situations, people usually do not have access to statistical information and thus are unfamiliar with incorporating such information when rendering judgment. They are, instead, exceedingly familiar with making decisions concerning individual cases. If someone needs a dentist, for example, friends are consulted and their advice is taken although their experience is unlikely to be the result of much probing for satisfactory dental care. Such proceeding would seem to be reasonable and rational decision making in situations in which statistical information about the quality of dentists' work is not available. When people are watching the news, however, focusing on a few selected individual cases, at the expense of attention to potentially more inclusive and therefore more reliable quantitative information, can no longer be considered reasonable. To the extent that recipients allow themselves to be more strongly influenced by a handful of individual cases than by available statistical information, they succumb to heuristic processing that manifests everyday rationality or common sense.

## The Availability Heuristic

The operation of this heuristic makes the perception and judgment of issues greatly dependent on the information that, for whatever reason, is presently available. Information that is accessed in memory at the time contemplation occurs thus is given disproportional influence on decision. For instance, a colleague's recent comment about the reliability of a product may, because of its recency, come to mind more readily than details of a consumer report read a month earlier; as a result, the remark may exert a greater degree of influence on the impression of the product's appeal than the detailed analysis. It is the currently available, presently accessed and activated information that is thought to have a stronger impact on judgment than potentially available, but momentarily dormant information.

In order to establish the operation of the availability heuristic, Tversky and Kahneman (1973) showed respondents lists containing the same number of men's and women's names. The list featured more famous women than famous men in one case. In the other, it featured more famous men than famous women. When the respondents were asked to estimate the percentage of males and females on the list, they overestimated the prevalence of women when the list was partial to famous women, and they overestimated the prevalence of men when the list favored famous men. Tversky and Kahneman (1973) explained this judgmental distortion as the result of easier retention of the names of famous persons. When asked to estimate the proportion of men and women, respondents apparently recalled the more famous names, and this recall conveyed an impression of greater multitude that biased their assessment. Based on research findings of this kind it may be concluded that information that is easily remembered because it has distinctive characteristics and can readily be pictured (or more generally, can be converted to sensory impressions) is likely to exert greater influence on judgment than would seem rational.

## Vividness and Salience

The operation of the availability heuristic is often expressed in terms of the vividness of information. It has been posited that the more vivid the information, the more influential its role in decision making. According to Nisbett and Ross (1980), vividness is determined chiefly by emotional interest, concreteness, and temporal and spatial proximity. In experimental situations, there are various techniques for generating vividness: the use of concrete, visual language (as opposed to abstract language); the use of photographs and film (as opposed to written material); direct experience (as opposed to vicarious experience through the media); and case-history information (as opposed to data summaries).

Taylor and Thompson (1982) gave similar accounts of the expected disproportional influence of vivid information displays. According to their reasoning, vivid information is retained more easily and to a greater degree, at least during the initial stages of processing. When rendering assessments of related situations at later times, vivid information displays come more readily to mind. Vivid displays are superior to others in creating concrete images of the objects being judged. Finally, vivid information displays tend to evoke stronger emotional reactions and foster more emotional involvement.

The empirical exploration of these projections of powerful vividness effects yielded rather disappointing results, however. On numerous occasions, psychologists have not been able to establish the expected stronger influence of vivid information displays. After a comprehensive review of the literature, Taylor and Thompson (1982) actually concluded that the effect of vivid information is comparatively weak (see also Brosius & Mundorf, 1990; Collins, Taylor, Wood, & Thompson, 1988; Kisielius & Sternthal, 1984, 1986). Vividness was found to have the predicted influence in only two of 23 studies. In 19 of the studies, appreciable effects could not be discerned, and in two further studies, nonvivid information (i.e., statistical accounts) was actually observed to have a stronger effect than vivid displays of concrete entities (i.e., parts of the statistical accounts).

One of the two investigations that could demonstrate the superior effect of vividly displayed information was conducted by Reyes, Thompson, and Bower (1980). These investigators simulated a court hearing in which either the plaintiff or the defendant used vivid arguments. Respondents were asked to recommend a sentence after the arguments had been presented. The sentence was harsher when the plaintiff had used vivid arguments and was less harsh when the defendant had used such arguments. Two days after hearing the case, this effect was found to be even stronger than immediately after exposure.

The inconsistencies in the findings concerning the impact of vividness seem to challenge not only common sense as based on everyday experience, but also are in discord with findings on the effects of the salience of information (cf. McArthur, 1981; Taylor & Fiske, 1975, 1978). *Salience,* a concept related to vividness, is commonly operationalized as an orienting motive that directs attention toward specific facets of the stimulus environment, usually but not necessarily those that have personal relevance. In a podium discussion, for instance, some participants may draw more attention than others because they are more conspicuous, either by their physique, their ethnicity, their clothing, or their mannerisms—or because they share the respondent's name or hairstyle. Taylor and Fiske (1978) categorized the conditions in which people or situations are perceived as "outstanding" and, in this sense, as extraordinary and important. These salient entities are said not to fit into existing contexts (e.g., a new student in class), to contradict expectations (e.g., behavior in violations of norms), or to be relevant to the goals of the observer (e.g., a superior). The findings of most investigations in this area show with considerable consistency that the portion of the perceived environment that draws the most attention, this being the salient portion, will have the strongest influence on recipients' judgment. It has been demonstrated, for example, that statements made by conspicuous persons are better retained than when made by less obtrusive others; as a result, they exert more influence on estimates of the prevalence of features and on assessments of the quality of matters under consideration.

Although vividness and salience have been operationalized in different ways, they are related concepts. Both concepts ascribe a central role to attention. Both seek to explain why certain stimulus displays are judged to be more relevant than others. In the case of vividness, greater relevance tends to be attributed to inherent qualities of informational displays. Vividness effects are thought to be mostly stimulus-driven. In the case of salience, in contrast, greater salience is primarily attributed to the recipients' orientation and disposition. It is considered driven by the environment–observer interaction. Examining the evidence on vividness effects in terms of this interaction makes it clear that the presumption of inherent, uniform stimulus quality is often untenable and that considerable individual variance is to be expected. Vividness studies that ignored the experience-based guidance of attention and its interpretative consequences thus may have been unproductive because of excessive error variance. Research employing the salience concept seems to have bypassed this problem by emphasizing experiential, subjective factors in selective attention and its judgmental consequences. Findings were more consistent as a result. Irrespective of these differences, however, both vividness and salience are highly useful concepts in that they elucidate the fickle function of selective attention in the perception and evaluation of objects, of persons, and of social issues.

The incorporation of these concepts in the availability heuristic is also most informative in considering mass-media phenomena. For instance, the false-consensus effect, manifest in people's belief that their own traits and opinions are more common than they actually are, can be explained as the result of people's superior access to their own traits and opinions (cf. Dawes, 1989; Hoch, 1987; Jonides & Naveh-Benjamin, 1987; MacLeod & Campbell, 1992; Marks & Miller, 1987). In similar fashion, priming can be explained as the result of superior accessibility of potentially available information. Priming simply enhances access to specific information that is pertinent to an issue to be appraised. The readily accessed information then has undue influence on the appraisal (Higgins & Chaires, 1980; Smith, 1988; Smith & Branscomb, 1987; Srull & Wyer, 1980; Wilson & Capitman, 1982). Iyengar and Kinder (1987) demonstrated this kind of influence for news reception specifically.

As attention mediators, vividness and salience are important not only within the availability heuristic; these mediators are also part and parcel of the representative heuristic in that they guide the perception of case attributes. Moreover, both heuristics share the principal assumptions that message recipients, especially in a media context, conduct neither exhaustive nor uniform appraisals of presented issues. Thoroughness usually gives way to expediency, and uniformity to varying personal beliefs and dispositions. At several stages in the reception process, particular and perhaps peculiar characteristics of the informational display will determine whether or not specific bits of information will be retained and used in the formation of judgments. Additionally, idiosyncratic dispositional factors will function as filters and will individualize attention, thereby pushing assessments further away from impartial, rational judgment.

Considering news reception, the distinction between exemplars (individual case histories) and base-rate information (quantification of reported cases) is of particular importance. Base-rate information is usually more comprehensive and valid, yet it lacks the vividness and probably the salience of exemplars that give them, according to numerous psychological investigations, greater influence on judgment. Giving credence to the indicated wealth of pertinent findings, it would appear that recipients liberally transfer the convenient and efficient heuristic ways of dealing with their immediate daily environment to the not-so-immediate world of the media. Such information processing clashes, of course, with idealized conceptions of the sciencelike, thoroughly rational scrutiny of issues. Recognition of this prompted Bargh (1984) to characterize the current Zeitgeist in social cognition as follows: ". . . a turn, in the middle of the last decade, away from the model of rational, scientific man and towards a model of man as cognitively limited and subject to all sorts of distortions, as a result" (p. 1).

### Chronic Accessibility

In recent developments that are especially important to the consideration of media effects, the availability heuristic has been refined by extension of the accessibility concept from comparatively short-lived contextual priming, which relies on the recency of construct activation, to *chronic accessibility,* which is defined as enduring accessibility that results from the potentially nonrecent frequent and consistent activation of particular constructs (Bargh, 1984; Bargh, Lombardi, & Higgins, 1988; Higgins, Bargh, & Lombardi, 1985).

Priming proper can be construed, in fact, as exceedingly short-lived, losing its influence as discursive changes manifest themselves. A rapidly changing discursive environment typifies, of course, the media context. Television, for instance, presents a continual flow of events. To the extent that these events define distinct priming constructs, a flow of different constructs is offered. This would seem to limit a prime's potential influence to the time prior to its being superseded by the presentation of another prime. The same limitation applies to the next prime, and so forth to the end of a presentation chain. In practical terms, a prime conveying the notion that random highway shooting is rampant may influence the perception of danger in skydiving, a sport featured in a subsequent report. On the other hand, this influence should terminate with the exhibition of joy from skydiving upon safe landing. The safe–joy message should be seen as a new prime capable of exerting contextual influence itself, proactively and even retroactively (cf. Mundorf & Zillmann, 1991; Zillmann, Gibson, Ordman, & Aust, 1994). The same applies to the priming influence of fiction (Jo & Berkowitz, 1994). A violence-laden film, for instance, might prime the notion that violence pays, as villains are witnessed enjoying the rewards of their actions. Eventually, however, as the perpetrators of criminal violence are brought to justice, the initial prime is replaced by a new one conveying the opposite construct.

The availability heuristic proper, especially when involving salience as an attention mediator, seems less time-dependent. Nonetheless, its reliance on the recency of construct activation also limits its influence over time, as it also is superseded by the influence of subsequently activated and therefore even more recent constructs. For instance, reports of a stock market crash may be salient to a point that "money lost" dominates information processing through the rest of the news. Then again, the later report of a killer tornado might draw sufficient attention to function as a newly activated "danger to life" construct that exerts its influence on whatever follows.

The indicated reconceptualization helps to overcome the limitations imposed by the reliance on the recency of construct activation. By focusing on frequent and consistent activation, it addresses the formation of persisting and ecologically more meaningful construct accessibility capable of influencing judgment for extended periods of time in essentially automatic fashion (Bargh, 1984; Bargh, Chaiken, Govender, & Pratto, 1992; Spielman, Pratto, & Bargh, 1988). Supportive research (Bargh et al., 1988; Higgins et al., 1985) suggests, in fact, that the nonimmediate influence of chronic accessibility on social judgment readily overwhelms that of contextual priming, the latter being dominant only immediately after construct activation.

Because it is commonly thought (cf. Gerbner, Gross, Morgan, & Signorielli, 1986; McCombs, 1994) that all significant media effects are built on frequent and consistent exposure to largely redundant concepts, this reconceptualization of accessibility in chronic, enduring terms holds great promise for the analysis of media influence. Perhaps most important, the concept of chronic accessibility, in contrast to conceptualizations such as schematic information processing, is operationally well articulated. Chronic accessibility seems sufficiently defined with the redundancy of construct presentations. Although the relative effect contribution of recency of exposure to that of frequency of exposure is left unspecified, the dominant influence ascribed to the frequency of concept exposure gives the chronic accessibility conceptualization great operational clarity. Additionally, because the conceptualization of chronic accessibility is mainly anchored in redundancy that is measurable in exposure frequency, it is bound to have great utility for the empirical exploration of media influence.

## EMOTION AS A MEDIATOR

Exemplars, as we have seen, differ in their capacity to avail or impose themselves from memory as related judgments are rendered. In the formation of chronic accessibility, their contributions must be expected to differ accordingly. The research evidence shows that perceptually vivid exemplars, compared to pallid ones, tend to foster superior accessibility. The lively imagery of an event, for instance, is bound to be more accessible than the drab verbal account of the event, both in the short run as well as in the long haul. Salience, the personal importance of an exemplified event, can be expected to exert a similar, if not stronger, influence on short-term or on long-term accessibility. Of perceptually equivalent exemplars, the one that touches the experiential history of persons or pertains to their desires and goals is bound to outdo the one that is devoid of such ramifications.

However, whereas much attention has been given to the vividness and salience of exemplars, the theorizing about heuristic information processing has largely ignored emotional reactivity and its potential influence on information storage, retrieval, and accessibility. This is surprising in view of the fact that a considerable amount of research exists on the influence of emotion on recall, and that, moreover, emotional reactivity can be construed as reactivity to especially salient stimuli. Consequently, we treat emotional reactivity as an integral part of salience.

The view that stimuli, exemplars included, that arouse the emotions are of greater personal significance than stimuli that leave recipients unruffled holds considerable intuitive appeal. Kety (1970) based a survival theory on this view, arguing that the recall of conditions that evoke emotions, especially fear, had adaptive value in the course of evolution, whereas the recall of conditions not prompting emotional reactions did not. Organismic sensitivity thus should favor the recall of information during emotion (Heuer & Reisberg, 1990). Remembering dangerous as compared to inconsequential situations had obviously greater utility and proved to be more adaptive for early humans, along with a multitude of other species. Having chronic access to the head shape and back pattern of poisonous snakes, for instance, was unquestionably more useful than having access to the visual particulars of flowers.

It can be considered firmly established that informational displays that evoke emotions are better recalled than those that do not—or that do so to a lesser degree (Christianson, 1992; Spear & Riccio, 1994). In fact, research focusing on emotional events and their recall has led to clearly articulated mechanisms for the mediation of superior accessibility. A structure within the limbic system, the amygdala, has emerged as the moderator that "computes" and signals the salience of events to the individual (LeDoux, 1992). This moderation actually manifests itself prior to the complete comprehension of imagery and text. In extreme emotions, imagery has been found to leave lasting vivid impressions, an effect that has been characterized as "flashbulb memory" (Brown & Kulik, 1977). More moderate emotions are associated with more moderate effects but still foster conditions that produce superior long-term storage of emotion-accompanying stimuli. Part and parcel of emotional reactivity is the release of adrenal catecholamines. This reaction lingers for several minutes, and it is during this period that the conditions for superior recall prevail (Bower, 1992). The emerging model for the creation of ready information access concerning events connected with the evocation of emotion (or events occurring during emotional arousal from potentially independent preceding emotions) is this: Amygdaloid monitoring prompts the discernment of exemplar salience that manifests itself, in part, in the activation of central norepinephrine receptors, and the enhanced sensitivity of these receptors creates the conditions for superior coding of emotional exemplars into indelible memory (Cahill, Prins, Weber, & McGaugh, 1994; McGaugh, 1992; McGaugh & Gold, 1989).

### Empathic and Counterempathic Reactivity

It might be argued that intense emotions capable of fostering indelible memory of the precipitating, accompanying, and subsequent circumstances are limited to extraordinary personal experiences, and that the media do not provide accounts and displays of events that are likely to evoke emotions of such intensity—at least not with regularity. The argument is in error, however, for a number of reasons.

First of all, the media can relate information about events that impacts the recipients' vital interests and welfare as directly as alternatively transmitted or immediately observed emotion-evoking events. For instance, reports of car thefts or of random shootings in the neighborhood are cases in point. Reports of stock market crashes and a failing world economy for those with money at stake, of a new wave of air terrorism for frequent and occasional flyers, and of long-range atomic or chemical weaponry in the hands of volatile and unpredictable governments for a nation in conflict with these governments, are all cases in point.

Second, recipients of media presentations are known to form alliances that are partly imaginary, such as in sportsfanship (Zillmann & Paulus, 1993) and in taste cultures (Zillmann & Gan, 1997), and that pursue seemingly playful objectives. Attaining these objectives or failing to do so, although not a matter of personal advancement or deprivation, tends to trigger exceedingly intense emotions of triumph and dejection nonetheless.

Third, similar but utterly serious factionalism exists in the political arena with the formation of dichotomies in terms of liberals and conservatives or simply along party lines. Any number of groupings are defined by specific vital interests. The elderly, for instance, are bound to respond emotionally to reports that place their continued financial support from Social Security in jeopardy. The young income earners who have to generate the necessary funds for this support might respond emotionally, too, although in a dramatically different way. Even seemingly trivial issues, such as the display of a nativity scene at the courthouse, can stir the emotions, though again in different directions, of Christians and of members of the ACLU (American Civil Liberties Union).

The point to be made is that the so-called mass-media audience is de facto composed of a multitude of interest groups in pursuit of ends they deem essential. News revelations are bound to touch on the objectives of at least some groups in the audience, on occasion on those concerning nearly the entire audience. The revelations thus will mean progress toward a goal for some and a setback of pursued objectives for others. Accordingly, they are likely to elicit joy in some and dejection in others. News revelations, if not entirely irrelevant, will touch the emotions of at least a good portion of the audience.

Finally, it is the portrayal of people that permeates media presentations of any kind. These people may be well known to the audience. Politicians, actors, athletes, and other celebrities define a familiar cast of public characters in the news and in quasi-news reporting. In fiction, characters are "developed" by their actions. In all of these cases the audience holds or ends up holding affective dispositions toward the fictional and nonfictional characters. Essentially, the individual members of the audience come to like particular characters and treat them in friendlike fashion; they come to dislike other characters and treat them like enemies; and they may remain affectively indifferent toward yet other characters and fail to care for them one way or the other.

It has been shown that these dispositions exert a powerful influence on emotional reactivity (Zillmann, 1991). Liking is known to elicit empathic responses. The success and joy of liked characters evokes hedonically compatible affective reactions. The success and joy of disliked characters, in contrast, is deplored and evokes hedonically opposite affective reactions. These reactions are said to be counterempathic. Moreover, characters toward whom dispositions of indifference are held fail to elicit appreciable emotions.

The mechanisms of these empathic, counterempathic, and nonempathic response tendencies are elaborated in drama theory and are supported by pertinent research evidence (Zillmann, 1994, 1996b). They also have been shown to apply to news reception, however (Zillmann, Taylor, & Lewis, 1998, 1999). Suffice it here to illustrate the applicability of empathy theory to affective reactions to news reports.

Zillmann et al. (1998, 1999) demonstrated, for instance, that the report of a leading politician's infliction with a venereal disease was applauded by those who hated him and deplored by those who loved him. The same set of responses was observed for the mishaps or setbacks befalling famous entertainers (i.e., actors and singers) and athletes. The hedonic response pattern predictably reversed for revelations of these public characters' good fortunes. These revelations prompted dejection in haters and applause in admirers. Regardless of the hedonic quality of the reaction, however, emotional intensity proved to be a function of the magnitude of affective disposition. Emotions, then, appear to be readily engaged by news revelations that are of no consequence for the personal welfare of the audience.

There are differences, nonetheless, in the evocation of emotional reactions by the news as compared to fiction. News revelations tend to confound, more strongly than fiction, the contributions to emotional reactivity by empathy and by prevailing contingencies of personal relevance. For instance, seeing the interview of a sympathetic old farmer, who recounts the experience of seeing his family get killed by a tornado, is likely to evoke emotional reactions. For recipients living in tornado-free regions, the reactions may be purely empathic. For those living in tornado-stricken regions, in contrast, the reactions may in part reflect activated concerns and fears of tornadoes. This probable confounding may actually explain the popular presumption that disaster accounts in the news liberate stronger emotions than those in fiction. This possibility notwithstanding, the news with its partiality to the coverage of all conceivable disasters (Haskins, 1984) tends to dwell on emotion-laden, gut-wrenching victim and bystander interviews. It is this circumstance that gives significance to the victim exemplar as an emotion inducer of potentially superior accessibility.

### Differently Diminishing Accessibilities

Few, if any, sensory experiences express themselves in permanently accessible exemplars (i.e., over a lifetime). Chronic accessibility may persist for weeks, months, and even years. However, such prolonged accessibility is subject to interference from related experiences, and this interference may result in the fading of initially imposing sensory impressions. Prolonged accessibility, then, is not permanent in a strict sense but may vary substantially in duration. Differences in the time course of the accessibility of exemplars have, of course, significant implications for the exemplars' influence on the perception and evaluation of phenomena.

First, it is to be expected that exemplars that consist of vivid stimulus displays, that are salient by pertaining to the recipients' welfare, and that elicit emotional reactions because of their salience, will have a longer "life span" than exemplars devoid of any or all of these qualities. The duration of exemplar influence on judgment should differ accordingly. For instance, the imagery of a totally disoriented, staggering cow in connection with a report on mad-cow disease may define an exemplar that strongly influences the judgment of the disease for months, if not years. A listless verbal specification of a cow's symptoms, in contrast, might yield an exemplar that becomes defunct after a few minutes or hours.

Second, the indicated discrepancy in the functional period of exemplars has significant implications for the influence of messages that aggregate numerous exemplars.

In the immediate effect of such messages, the influence of exemplars can be considered to merge. All exemplars are accessible, but some are bound to be more imposing than others. On the whole, however, the contribution of the exemplars to an overall impression of the addressed phenomenon can be considered to sum to a total.

This is not at all the case for delayed effects. In these effects, short-lived exemplars have dropped out, along with their influence on perception and on judgment. The more potent, persisting exemplars now attain disproportionate influence. In rendering judgment, they now constitute the focal point. In defining focus, they may revive related information, thereby drawing even more attention to the informational facet that they represent. For instance, recipients of an image-laden broadcast on the mad-cow disease who encounter the issue again a year after seeing the broadcast may now form their assessment of the disease primarily on the basis of the imagery—as they cannot retrieve much else that was said or shown about it. The influential power of vivid, salient, and emotional exemplars thus does not necessarily manifest itself immediately but should be expected to materialize and potentially grow over time.

The suggested mashing of exemplar influence, especially regarding the dominance of the perceptually stronger and more specific exemplars over the weaker and vaguer ones, has been demonstrated. Grimes (1990), for instance, has shown that the information presented in text–image admixtures tends to combine and fuse with the passage of time. In a paradigm-setting study, Pezdek (1977) observed that the information of simultaneously presented verbal statements (e.g., "The bird was perched atop the tree.") and images (e.g., of an eagle perched atop a tree) merged over time (i.e., respondents believed the sentence to have been "An eagle was perched atop the tree."). Grimes applied this research paradigm to a television news report in which statements coincided with particular images. In a report on dating services, the text stated, for instance, that daters do not reveal many of their vices. The simultaneously presented imagery showed a student with a gin bottle in his back pocket. After a 2-day delay, respondents recalled the text as essentially stating that daters do not reveal their alcoholism, among other vices.

Most effects of this kind can be derived from dual-coding theory (Paivio, 1971, 1986). Essentially, this theory posits that mental representations retain properties of the evocative external stimulation. Linguistic and nonlinguistic events are therefore presumed to be independently stored as *logogens* and *imagens,* respectively. Logogens and imagens are thought to be strongly interconnected, however. Representational integration is presumed to be automatic (i.e. nonconscious) and dominated by imagens, especially over time. The well-documented picture-superiority effect of information acquisition (Madigan, 1983; Paivio, Rogers, & Smythe, 1968) pertains to this imagen dominance.

Alternative models of information coding (e.g., Collins & Loftus, 1975; Klatzky, 1980; Kosslyn, 1978, 1983) do not assume separate but interconnected image storing. They do emphasize, however, the dominance of specific, concrete over more general, abstract information, thus allowing the derivation of similar effect expectations.

## CONTINGENCY PROCESSING

Social learning theory (Bandura, 1969, 1971, 1986) pertains to exemplification because it focuses on the intra-exemplar connection between displayed actions and their observed, inferred, or presumed consequences. From this linkage, the proposal that behaviors, along with their motivating beliefs and dispositions, can be acquired by observation alone (i.e., without repeated overt action under relevant circumstances) is derived. The proposal applies to media presentation of behavior–

consequence contingencies as much as to the direct observation of these contingencies. As a result, it is vital for the consideration of media effects on behavior and its motivating conditions.

Because the paradigm of observational, no-trial learning concentrates on what is contingent on the performance of particular behaviors by others, it is not limited to projecting effects on impressions of prevalence or typicality of observed behavior, but it also addresses consequences such as the desirability and undesirability of the observed behavior by the observer. For instance, a child's observation of another child's aggressive play (e.g., pulling and snapping the nose of a toy clown) may foster a degree of curiosity but may be inconsequential for the onlooking child's motivation and behavior. Observing a relevant consequence of the play, in contrast, should enhance or diminish this onlooking child's desire for playing similarly. If such play were observed to yield rewards (i.e., incentives from a third party or the model's expression of great pleasure), the desire to imitate (or in behavioral terms, the imitation rate) should increase. If it were observed to yield aversive, punitive consequences, the desire to imitate should decline, instead. Bandura and his coworkers (cf. Bandura, 1986) have generated ample research evidence for the outlined operation of observed contingencies of reinforcement and punishment.

## The Informative Function

Bandura (e.g., 1971) proposed two principal mechanisms to explain such effects of observed contingencies between behavior and its yield. The first one is the *informative function* of observed outcomes. It suggests that witnessing the consequences of others' behavior makes observers cognizant of prevailing contingencies of reinforcement and punishment, and that this cognizance allows them to arrange their own behavior so as to maximize rewards and minimize aversions in the same and similar environments—all without having directly experienced these contingencies. The generalization to similar social environments is obviously limited by personal experience with the contingencies in question. Observers who know that the contingencies do not apply to particular environments are in a position to resist generalizing. Those who do not have this knowledge, in contrast, are expected to assume that the contingencies apply and to arrange their actions accordingly. According to the informative-function proposal, then, it is the anticipation of consequences based on the immediate or mediated observation of the behavior of others, rather than personal experience, that guides dispositions and actions. As Bandura (1971) put it, "Unlike the operant conditioning interpretation, the social learning formulation assumes that imitative behavior is regulated by observers' judgments of probable consequences for prospective actions rather than being directly controlled by stimuli that were correlated with reinforcement" (p. 49).

In support of this proposal it has been shown (e.g., Bandura & Barab, 1971; Kaufman, Baron, & Kopp, 1966) that contingencies of reinforcement and of punishment that are believed to prevail do indeed control behavior. It has been observed, in fact, that contingencies believed to prevail are capable of overriding and dominating the controlling influence of the actually prevailing contingencies.

The informative-function proposal is readily incorporated in exemplification considerations. The only requirement is to broaden the conceptualization of exemplars of observed behavior. These exemplars can be considered to carry with them information about consequences of the behavior, with these consequences applying to others and to self. For instance, seeing a person smoke a cigar with gusto constitutes contingency processing instigated by an exemplar of a cigar smoker with a joy tag added to the smoking. The verbal equivalent would not merely be "person smoking a cigar," but "person enjoying smoking a cigar." Exposure to many such contingency exemplars may not simply give the impression that cigar smoking is popular among those exemplified, but may foster anticipations of enjoyment and may ultimately tempt observers to attain similar pleasure by smoking a cigar. In fact, contingency exemplars might influence them to a point where, in order to avoid feeling deviant, they have to talk themselves into liking the experience when, in fact, they do not. A counterexemplar showing a person having coughing fits from cigar smoking should, of course, tag displeasure rather than pleasure in connection with the behavior; and it should not only give the impression that some fail to attain pleasure, but it should not tempt observers to try because of the anticipated possibility of displeasure.

The expression of pleasure or of displeasure in connection with particular behaviors constitutes only one of numerous manifestations of relevant consequences. Success in dating, professional advancement, the attainment of fame and fortune, but also the convenience of achieving valued objectives, are all incentives that may accrue to exemplars of behavior. American beer commercials, for instance, traditionally depict average men who consume a specific brand as being irresistible to gorgeous women. The fact that the use of this theme never dies would seem to suggest at least minimal effectiveness of the campaigns employing this theme. The contingency appears to be uncritically accepted as a causal relation (i.e., consumption creating appeal), because only if such credence exists should observers become inclined to seek the "indirect benefits" of consuming a particular brand of beer.

In recent antismoking campaigns, efforts have been made to undo the effects of decades of exemplifying cigarette smoking as providing satisfaction and enhancing appeal. Oddly, these efforts simply reverse the sexual-appeal association. They exemplify the instant cessation of the heterosexual appeal of attractive men upon their lighting up a cigarette.

These illustrations should suffice in showing that advertising is permeated with behavior exemplifications whose purpose becomes meaningful only after contingency coding is considered. Such coding is not limited to deliberate persuasive efforts, however, but also permeates the news and fiction.

The news, for instance, by exemplifying violent criminals as members of specific ethnic groups, is likely to foster the impression that members of these ethnic groups are violent and dangerous. To the extent that this exemplification is biased, such impressions are bound to be biased as well. In fiction, moreover, the frequent portrayal of particular sexual practices can be expected to foster the impression of their excessive popularity and to entice imitation in addition. Exemplar-evoked anticipations of the enjoyment of specific actions, along with admiration for their performance, should at least on occasion lead to overt behavior. Such influence of nonfictional and fictional exemplification should be characteristic in behavioral domains devoid of opposing personal experience. It should be minimal in domains where anticipations are founded on experience with the contingencies in question. It should be clear as well that media influence, as it generates temptations, may prompt probing, but is limited to a trial or two whenever anticipations are thwarted. Disappointment can be seen as the ultimate corrective for behavior resulting from exemplification-evoked anticipations.

## Affect Enhancement

The second principal mechanism of social learning (Bandura, 1971, 1986) concerns emotional reactivity by empathy as *vicarious affect*. It applies to contingency exemplars in that they tend to feature not only the rewarding or punitive consequences of actions but also the agents' affective responses to these consequences. The evocation of appreciable empathic and counterempathic reactions is to be expected. These reactions, as indicated earlier, are likely to facilitate retention and retrieval of the exemplar. The focus of observational learning is not so much on information accessibility and its influence on judgment, however, as it is on disposition formation, response preparation, and imitative action.

More specifically, it is assumed that expectations of pleasure versus displeasure, success versus failure, safety versus danger, and the like that derive from the informative function of social learning are potentiated by accompanying emotional arousal (cf. Zillmann, 1996a). Imitative desire or avoidance motivation should increase proportionally with the intensity of positive or negative affect, respectively. It is this extension of purely cognition-based expectations to motivated actions and their potential execution that social learning theory provides.

In practical terms, attention to emotional reactivity leads to the proposal that the effect of contingency exemplars on dispositions and on associated behaviors will be stronger the more these exemplars engaged the emotions. Responding emotionally to a lottery winner's jumping for joy, for instance, should entice observers to try their own luck at playing the lottery more than should responding unexcitedly to the plain announcement of the winner's good fortune. Likewise, responding emotionally to learning about the suffering of motorists who were shot by a sniper from a bridge across the interstate is likely to foster stronger apprehensions and more weariness in motorists using this part of the interstate than is the nonemotional acquisition of information about the simple fact of the shooting.

## Model–Observer Affinity

Social learning theory (Bandura, 1986) is of further value in the consideration of exemplar effects because it emphasizes the affinity between exemplified persons and observers. The affinity in question is defined along various dimensions of perceived attributes of others and of self, such as gender, ethnicity, age, education, profession, economic standing, and social status. It is posited that observers, in paying attention to and empathizing with persons in exemplars, are generally partial to those with whom they share the largest number of attributes. In other words, they side, as a rule, with "their own kind." It is expected, for instance, that boys watch and do what other boys do, and that the rich and famous take cues from, and tend to imitate the actions of, those who exhibit their own characteristics.

Although much research supports this partiality to similar and to like persons (Bandura, 1986; Higgins, 1996), there are at least two notable exceptions to the affinity rule. First, heterosexual interest is known to foster selective attention to the opposite gender, without the intent to behave similarly. Second, persons often strive to improve their social standing and on occasion sacrifice model–observer affinity in the process. The *actual self* is denied in favor of the *ideal self* (Higgins, 1989), and selective attention is paid to the behavior of those who approximate the ideal self. Desired and anticipated socialization potentially fosters the emulation of idealized exemplified persons.

Social learning theory also addresses attraction to conspicuousness and the exceptionality of models. This condition has been amply considered, however, in connection with the vividness and the atypicality of exemplars.

# FOUR

# Exemplification Effects of the News

The news media, as they provide quantitative information in the form of general or specific base-rate information about phenomena, obviously attempt to influence the perception of quantitative aspects of these phenomena. Less obvious is that the provision of a few case descriptions may have a similar, and on occasion even stronger, influence on the perception of quantitative manifestations—although this influence may come about inadvertently. Whether deliberate or inadvertent, the influence of news reports, mostly composites of base-rate information and exemplars, on the recipients' perception of quantitative aspects of phenomena has been explored in numerous investigations.

## FOCI OF EXPLORATION

The perception under consideration has been ascertained with three distinct foci: the perception of incidence rates (i.e., the ratio of specific manifestations within a set of manifestations of interest), the perception of the magnitude of opportunities and risks to others (i.e., to specific groups or to the public at large), and the perception of the magnitude of opportunities and risks to self.

First, impressions of quantitative aspects of phenomena have been measured in the perceptions, or more precisely in estimates, of the number or the proportion of persons in a social grouping who hold particular beliefs and dispositions, as well as behave in certain ways. Impressions of minorities and of majorities, or simply the degree of prevalence or scarcity of entities, are typically expressed in percentages of a larger aggregate of persons or of entities, implying that the entities considered are part of an identified whole. For instance, people voting Republican can be quantified as a percentage of voters as a whole. Violent carjackings, likewise, constitute a ratio of carjackings as a whole, and black tulips constitute a ratio of tulips as a whole. Impressions of incidence rates may also be measured on ordinal scales (e.g., from none and few to many and all). This is rarely done, however, mostly because of statistical considerations (i.e., loss of power in analyses).

Second, in contrast to the indicated estimation of incidence distributions, phenomena can be judged in terms of perceived magnitude. Both opportunities and risks can be measured in perceived likelihoods, for instance. Recipients tend to think in terms of "chances are . . ." that things might or will happen to them or to others. As the news is partial to reporting dangers, research has largely bypassed opportunity perceptions. Risk perceptions have been the center of attention, with perceived risk to self and to others being measured in probability estimates (e.g., How likely do you think it is that . . . can or will happen to . . . ?). However, risk has also been measured in terms of perceived magnitude (i.e., in ratings between nil and extreme on ratio scales). Ordinal measures were again avoided in the interest of statistical power.

Conceptually, the second focus in perception assessment concerns risk (or opportunity) to the public or to a defined subsection thereof. The third focus in perception assessment involves the same measures of risk (or opportunity) but concerns the self. Risk perceptions are known to foster the formation of protective dispositions and to correlate with these dispositions (Sawyer, Kernan, Conlon, & Garland, 1999). As a result, protective dispositions, and on occasion overt protective behaviors, are employed as indirect measures of risk perception.

Given these foci on the perceptual, dispositional, and behavioral influence of exemplification, the effects of the following news variables were investigated:

1. precise and imprecise base-rate information (relative to exemplar aggregation),
2. quantitatively distinct aggregation of exemplars and counterexemplars,

3. qualitatively distinct exemplar aggregation,
4. employment of emotion-evoking exemplars, and
5. employment of pictorial exemplars (relative to verbal exemplars).

It should be clear that the focus on particular aspects of influence determines the degree to which research findings pertain to broad conceptions of media influence. Findings concerning the perception of incidence rates, for instance, pertain to public-opinion theories such as the spiral of silence (Noelle-Neumann, 1980). This theory posits that opinions of minorities that are with some regularity voiced in public are perceived to be more widespread than they actually are; as a result, people are more predisposed to support the overestimated minority position than they would without distorted perception. According to Noelle-Neumann, the media play an important role in this process by providing information about minorities and majorities and their opinions. Frequent reports or exemplifications of the minority position by the media, along with a relative neglect of the majority position, is seen as initiating and eventually completing a minority-to-majority shift in public opinion.

The perception of incidence rates is also of importance to media influence in terms of the cultivation proposal (Gerbner, Gross, Morgan, & Signorielli, 1986). The distribution of those holding power to those being deprived of it, for instance, would be pertinent, as would be the prevalence of those posing danger to the public. Consideration of the threat of violent victimization, however, shifts the focus from incidence perception to risk perception. Exemplification of danger by the news as well as in fiction, the so-called scary world of television, is expected to foster, in the end, personal apprehensions about becoming a victim of violent crime. The reasoning, then, spans the perception of the incidence of victimization, the perception of the risk of victimization to others, and lastly the perception of the personal risk of victimization that may express itself in feelings of apprehension, in fear of strangers, in protective dispositions, and in cautious habits—such as the deliberate circumvention of places and times associated with heightened risk. It thus cuts across perceptual, judgmental, dispositional, experiential, and behavioral effects, all of which are deemed intercorrelated.

Suffice it here to suggest that exemplification is an integral, albeit unacknowledged, component of such influence projections. We shall not attempt, however, to incorporate the effect mechanisms of exemplification in the indicated theories or similar proposals (e.g., agenda setting; McCombs, 1994). Instead, we focus on what is known about the influence of different exemplifications manifest in news reporting (or in fiction and in quasi-fiction; see chapter 5). To the extent that the research evidence is consistent with, and in this sense supportive of, the exemplar effect mechanisms that have been discussed in chapter 3, these mechanisms may, of course, be presumed operative in the influence of the media generally. They consequently should, in one form or another, enter into any comprehensive theory of media effects.

defensive reaction

A comment on risk assessment is in order. Based on the so-called third-person effect of media influence (Davison, 1983) which projects greater influence perception for others than for self, it might be expected that the assessment of others' risks yields generally higher estimates than that of personal risks. Such a conclusion would seem to be premature, however.

The third-person effect of media influence is not in doubt. It has been demonstrated with considerable consistency (Perloff, 1993). It has been observed, for instance, for the influence of pornography (Gunther, 1995), the susceptibility in considering a murder suspect guilty or not (Driscoll & Salwen, 1997), the effect on attitudes toward politicians (Price, Huang, & Tewksbury, 1997), consequences for idealized person perception (David & Johnson, 1998), and acquiescence in editorial decision making (Price, Tewksbury, & Huang, 1998). The common feature of these investigations is that they specifically address media influence, essentially querying, "How much would this message influence you?" "How much would it influence others (usually the public)?" Cynics might contend that the question indirectly asks, "How gullible are you compared to others?" If so questioned, the stronger denial of personal gullibility, along with the ascription of greater gullibility to those others, should not be surprising.

An investigation by White (1997) lends some credence to this interpretation. This investigator observed a third-person effect for the judged persuasiveness of messages composed of weak arguments. Judging the persuasiveness of messages featuring strong arguments produced the opposite result. Respondents apparently thought others not only more gullible than themselves in succumbing to poor argumentation, but they also considered themselves intellectually superior to others in comprehending convincing argumentation.

Gunther and Mundy (1993) held a self-serving, optimistic bias accountable for third-person effects. In agreement with their findings (as well as with the gullibility rationale), these investigators argued that:

> People are likely to consider themselves smarter and more resistant to a message when they feel the topic is one that has little benefit, or even potentially harmful consequences, for its audience. If the potential benefit from a message is high, however, then people consider themselves just as much influenced as others. In some cases, they may anticipate even more effect on themselves. (p. 66)

This suggestion limits the third-person effect to influence entailing potential harm or, at least, no benefits. It makes the effect a function of message content and thereby denies its universality. On the other hand, the suggestion implies that, in connection with the salience of harm, the perception of risk is centrally involved.

Brosius and Engel (1996), in examining the mediation of the third-person effect, extracted unrealistic optimism as the primary factor of several mediating factors. This factor is again linked to risk perception. The implicated mechanism essentially projects that persons, who by acknowledging message influence would recognize and admit their own vulnerability, rather deny influence (to a degree) in the interest of maintaining a favorable self-appraisal, illusory as it may be. Such defensive pressures would not exist in the assessment of others' risk.

There is every reason to believe that defensive misappraisals of this sort are also operative in the assessment of personal risks relative to the risks of others (cf. Taylor, Wayment, & Collins, 1993). It should be clear, however, that likely third-person effects in this domain do not concern a difference in perceived media influence; rather, they express a specific difference in perceived risk to self and to others that may or may not be modified by media influence. In these risk assessments, the query is not "How much influence . . . ?" but rather "How great a risk . . . ?"

In considering third-person effects of risk perception (not of media-influence perception), defensive distortions in the assessment of personal risks may well yield higher assessments of others' risks in a majority of cases. It should not be considered to be the rule, however. In contrast to assessing message influence, with respondents usually guessing (as they have no basis for sound judgment), persons tend to know their own vulnerabilities relative to those of others, often in rather precise terms. For instance, persons living in smoggy Los Angeles are likely to be cognizant of their risk of eventually developing respiratory complications and, as a consequence, rate their personal risk higher than that of the general population. Those living in "Big Sky" country, having little cause for considering themselves at respiratory risk, should provide reversed ratings. The latter has the appearance of a third-person effect, but not for reasons associated with defensive correction. The situation is similar for persons living in the so-called tornado alley as compared to those living in areas where tornadoes are not known to occur. Only the former group is likely to assess their risk above that of the general population. Risk, however, may also be constitutionally defined. Persons cognizant of their high blood pressure are likely to consider themselves at higher risk of heart attack than the population at large; similarly, especially fragile elderly persons may recognize their vulnerability and consider themselves at greater risk than others of being mugged (cf. Perloff, 1983).

Essentially, then, it may be assumed that people perceive themselves to be at either no, low, moderate, high, or extreme risk concerning particular threats, and that they consider others at lesser, at similar, or at higher risk than themselves. Comparative ratings, to the extent that they are free of defensive, self-serving distortions, thus may yield greatly varied outcomes.

## THE RESEARCH EVIDENCE

As already indicated in chapter 3, the relative influence of base-rate information versus that of the involvement of exemplars has been examined in various psychological investigations. Initial findings reported by Kahneman and Tversky (1973), by Hammerton (1973), and by Lyon and Slovic (1976) gave evidence that people often, and in gross violation of rationality assumptions, neglected reliable base-rate data and based their quantitative assessments on the less reliable but more specific and concrete information expressed in exemplars. The dominant influence of exemplification is especially surprising in view of the fact that the investigations in question pitted base-rate information against just one exemplar. Lyon and Slovic (1976), for instance, presented information about taxis, about a hit-and-run accident, and about the reliability of an eyewitness in a quizlike format to their respondents. Specifically, the ratio of green to blue taxis was provided, along with the witness' ability to distinguish the colors. When asked to estimate the probability that the accident-causing cab was blue, the respondents relied on the witness and largely ignored the known distribution of taxis.

The aforediscussed investigation by Hamill and colleagues (1980) does not have such artificiality of format, but still relies on a singular exemplar. It is also worthy of note that base-rate information was not specifically quantitative. It was comparatively vague, merely specifying the typicality or the atypicality of the singular case. In this investigation, respondents read a news report about a person (such as an irresponsible welfare recipient) and then indicated dispositions toward the population from which this person was drawn. Prior to or after reading the report, they were exposed to an editorial note stating that the described case was either typical or atypical. The declaration of atypicality amounts to stating that the case is nonrepresentative and should be discounted in the appraisal of the population. No such effect was observed. Respondents were influenced by the case, generalizing it to the population (this effect being relative to a control condition in which the news report was not read). The base-rate qualifications, whether presented before or after the reading of the article, proved to be inconsequential.

Hamill and colleagues (1980) interpreted their findings as evidence of the ready neglect of pallid base-rate information as well as of the power of a single concrete and vivid exemplar. Perhaps more important is the fact that their investigation, as it appears to have great ecological validity, defined the format for most subsequent media research on exemplification.

### Exemplar–Counterexemplar Distributions

Research on the influence of exemplars soon moved beyond single-case descriptions and elaborated the exemplification concept. In efforts at attaining high degrees of ecological validity, it involved types and distributions of exemplars that are characteristically employed in media presentations, in news reporting in particular. The comparison of the influence of base-rate information with that of exemplars was retained for some time, however. In addition, the duration of the effects of these two principal message components became a significant issue. It did so because of the hypothesized growing dominance of the superior accessibility of concrete, vivid over abstract, pallid information and its corresponding influence on judgment.

Zillmann, Perkins, and Sundar (1992) conducted an investigation in which they varied the precision of base-rate information, the ratio of exemplars to counterexemplars, and the time of issue assessment after exposure. Specifically, a report on weight regaining after successful dieting, presented as a one-page Special Report from *Newsweek*, started with a case description, provided base-rate information, and then featured eight more case descriptions. It was titled "Keeping off Weight: The Battle with Diet Plans." The news release of a research institute provided the base-rate information. It was reported either that, of the dieters who successfully lose weight during a diet program, 32% would regain the lost weight within a year's time (precise base rate), or that a minority of them would regain the lost weight in this period (vague base rate). The nine exemplars featured interviews with dieters who, consistent with the article's focus, managed to control their weight (i.e., keeping it off), or dieters who, counter to this focus, had regained the lost weight. For instance, a focus-consistent exemplar was the following:

A year has passed for Jann Fabrizio of Milwaukee, Wis., and she only dreams of size six dresses and morning jogs around a lake near her home. She lost 110 pounds on a diet program and after a year, she has gained back all the weight. "I just couldn't continue keeping those detailed food records and exercising," she explains. "I can't keep doing that for the rest of my life."

A counterexemplar was the following:

T. Edgar Jamison of Oak Ridge, Tenn., shed 114 pounds in a year using a popular program. He said his health improved because he has maintained his weight. His thyroid system is in sync and he now can climb stairs without panting. "The doctor said chances are good my thyroid will remain normal, and the damage to my body will be repaired," Edgar said. "I paid the price. I have energy to run a mile again, play basketball, and go swimming with my children."

In order to ascertain the effects of different exemplar aggregations, three specific ratios of focus-consistent to focus-inconsistent exemplars were created. In *selective,* entirely focus-driven exemplification, all nine exemplars portrayed persons who managed to keep their weight under control—the one third minority, according to the precise base-rate information. In *representative* exemplification, three focus-consistent exemplars were interspersed among six counterexemplars. This presentation thus featured a proportionally correct representation of the distribution of cases reported in the news release. It should be clear that such representation, because it is often not feasible, constitutes an ideal. A more viable alternative to selective exemplification is to at least acknowledge the existence of counterexemplars. This alternative was created by reversing the proportion of exemplars to counterexemplars. In *blended* exemplification, then, the majority was underrepresented (three exemplars) and the minority was overrepresented (six exemplars). The impression of a complete absence of counterexemplars, as invited by selective exemplification, was avoided, however.

Respondents read three news reports on different issues, one being the manipulated report on weight regaining. All were queried about their own perceptions of the issues addressed in two of the reports. In the no-delay condition, they were tested shortly after reading on the regaining of lost weight. In the delay condition, this assessment was omitted, and respondents were queried on the issue 14 days after reading the weight article. This was done without forewarning (i.e., the test came as a surprise). Respondents were asked to indicate their own beliefs about the so-called yo-yo phenomenon of weight loss and the regaining of weight. Specifically, they were asked to estimate the number of people who, after losing weight, would regain it in a year's time.

It was expected, first of all, that the estimates of those who had been provided with precise base-rate information should be less influenced by discrepant exemplification than the estimates of those who had been exposed to vague base-rate information. That is, in case of a discrepancy between base-rate data and exemplar distribution, precision should assert a stronger influence than vagueness; in case of compatibility between base-rate data and exemplification, especially representative exemplification, the precision of base-rate information should be immaterial. The indicated interaction was not observed, however. Instead, a main effect of base-rate precision was attained, indicating that, overall, the provision of precise base-rate information yielded estimates that were somewhat less erroneous than those based on vague base-rate statements.

More important, it was expected that base-rate information, especially when precise, would be well recalled shortly after reading and consequently would then exert strong influence on perception. This influence was presumed strong enough to dominate the potential influence of exemplar aggregation. Moreover, it was expected that this influence pattern would reverse for the delayed assessment of estimates. After 14 days, the specifics of the general, abstract information were presumed to be largely forgotten. Impressions created by the concrete exemplars should be better retained and now come to dominate judgment.

The pertinent findings, presented in Table 4.1, do not at all support these predictions. As can be seen, base-rate information proved to be immaterial, especially shortly after being read. It did not prevent the effect of exemplification. This effect shows gross overestimation of the incidence of weight regaining after exposure to selective exemplification (three fourths of dieters, with one third being correct). The presentation of nine exemplars on the regainer side thus entirely overpowered the specification of actual percentages or vaguer indications of prevalence. Representative exemplification produced the best approximation of correct assessment, although this assessment also proved to be too high. Blended representation fostered, as expected, assessments of intermediate accuracy.

The findings concerning delayed assessments also disconfirmed expectations. Instead of showing the differentiation observed for immediate assessment, they indicate the complete dissipation of the initial effect. It was speculated that, over time, respondents in the delay condition regressed to beliefs about weight loss and

TABLE 4.1
Percentage Estimates of Weight Regainers as a Function
of Relative Frequency of Exemplification in a Print-News Report
and Time of Assessment After Reading

| | Exemplar Conditions | | |
|---|---|---|---|
| Time of Assessment | Selective | Blended | Representative |
| No delay | $75.0^{Aa}$ | $62.3^{Ba}$ | $58.5^{Bb}$ |
| 14-day delay | $70.2^{Aa}$ | $69.2^{Aa}$ | $73.8^{Aa}$ |

*Note.* Smaller scores indicate greater accuracy of estimates. Comparisons across exemplar conditions are specified by uppercase superscripts, comparisons across time of assessment by lowercase superscripts. Means having different superscripts differ significantly at $p < .05$. Authors' data, first published in "Impression-formation effects of printed news varying in descriptive precision and exemplifications," by D. Zillmann, J. W. Perkins, and S. S. Sundar, 1992, *Medienpsychologie: Zeitschrift für Individual- und Massenkommunikation,* 4(3), 168–185, 239–240.

regaining that were held prior to reading the article. Subsequent testing showed, in fact, that persons who had not read the article severely overestimated the incidence of weight regaining at 72%. The mean of estimates in the delay conditions was 71%. This convergence not only gives credence to the explanation that respondents reverted to initial beliefs, but it also explains the surprisingly high estimates in all other conditions.

In summary, then, the findings of this investigation show that different aggregations of exemplars in news reports are capable of producing specific, predictable effects on the perception of relevant issues. Specifically, the perception of general incidence rates appears to follow the rates of exemplified cases. The observed short-term effects materialized in the presence of divergent precise or vague base-rate information, attesting to the earlier reported lack of appreciable influences of such competing information. As no delayed effects could be demonstrated, the findings suggest, moreover, that for issues that are associated with established prior beliefs, the short-term effects of exemplification diminish, and persons eventually revert to their prior beliefs. The exact duration of the short-term effects under these conditions remains unclear, however.

Brosius (1995, 1996; see also Brosius & Bathelt, 1994) conducted a series of six experiments that examined the effects of variations in the number and the distribution of exemplars representing either the majority or the minority stand on issues, the vividness of the exemplars (vivid vs. pallid language), the precision of the base-rate information (absolute vs. relative), the medium of presentation (radio vs. print), and the time of perception assessment (immediately vs. a delay of 1 week). All participants in the experiments were presented with a series of four stories on different issues. The issues varied in terms of salience (two were pertinent to the participants, two were not) and of focus (two related to technical issues, two related to food or beverage preferences).

A radio program was created, consisting of a header jingle, a reporter's introduction to the program, four stories on topics of local or regional interest, and a trailer jingle. The program was produced in a local radio station using professional reporters and equipment. All four stories were put together in a similar fashion. At the outset, the anchor introduced an issue (e.g., the alleged decreasing quality of the apple wine in the region around Frankfurt, Germany). This was followed by the presentation of base-rate information about the people involved in the issue (e.g., apple wine drinkers) who were holding favorable or unfavorable opinions (e.g., "only a few people still like the apple wine"). Finally, the anchor introduced a reporter on location. In the concluding part of the story, this reporter interviewed a number of persons who indicated their opinion about the issue (e.g., they said that they like or dislike the apple wine).

The first story concerned the replacement of coin-operated public telephones with prepaid-card telephones in a nearby town. The base-rate information identified the large majority of the town's citizens as opposing the introduction of card telephones. The second story dealt with the quality of cafeteria food at a university in a neighboring city. The base-rate information indicated that the large majority of students did not like the food. The third story dealt with the quality of the traditional apple wine in the Frankfurt region. The base-rate information stated that only a minority would still be satisfied with the quality of the wine. The last story concerned the introduction of obligatory computer courses for every university student, with the base-rate information showing the large majority of students in favor of such obligatory courses. Opinions about the issues of the first and the fourth story thus varied in terms of approve–disapprove; those about the issues of the second and third stories varied in terms of like–dislike.

University students served as respondents. In order to disguise the actual purpose of the research, respondents were asked to help evaluate the quality and appropriateness of news reports produced by fellow students, this in anticipation of services to be provided by a new student radio station. Additionally, the radio programs were converted into printed reports, and students who read these reports were told that the indicated services would be provided by a new student newspaper. After hearing or reading a report, respondents evaluated its quality, moved on to the next, and so forth. Following the evaluation of all four reports, they indicated their opinions on different issues, including those that had been presented in the reports.

An additional experimental variation involved repeated and delayed opinion assessments. Specifically, half of the respondents reported their opinions immediately after report exposure. For the other half, the immediate assessment was omitted (as detailed in connection with the investigation by Zillmann et al., 1992) and opinions were assessed 1 week after exposure.

The final investigation, employing print-magazine reports, involved two new stories in addition to those on the introduction of card telephones and the quality of apple wine. The new stories dealt with the plan of creating a traffic-free pedestrian zone in a German town and with tele-shopping. In the antitraffic story, the base-rate information projected that the majority of the citizenry was in opposition to the plan. Accompanying the survey were interviews either of four persons opposing the pedestrian zone versus one person favoring it (base rate consistent) or four persons favoring it versus one person in opposition to it (in contradiction to the base rate). The tele-shopping story described the successful operation of a new shopping system that allows the ordering of merchandize via television, along with prompt home delivery. The lead emphasized that this service was strongly applauded by most citizens (base-rate information). Interviews again presented either four persons supporting and one person opposing the system (base rate consistent) or four persons opposing and one person supporting it (in contradiction to the base rate).

The perceived quality of the reports was ascertained by ratings of credibility and of vividness, along with other story aspects. The research focus was, of course, on the measurement of the perceived distribution of opinions as well as the respondents' own views. Two questions were asked for each story. In case of the cafeteria-food story, for instance, the first question addressed the opinion distribution: "The report described the quality of the cafeteria food. According to the report, what was the percentage of students who were satisfied with the food?" The second question asked for the respondents' own opinions: "In your opinion, is the quality of the cafeteria food rather good or rather bad?"

The first experiment employed a three-factor design varying the distribution of exemplars, the vividness of exemplar language, and the originator of the exemplars. The base-rate information stated that the majority of people would favor obligatory computer courses. Consistent exemplification featured the interviews of four persons supporting the introduction of such courses and one person opposing it. The number of supporting and opposing persons was reversed for inconsistent exemplification. The interview language was altered to create vivid versus pallid expression. In the vivid version, the interviewed persons' language was emotional and accentuated; in the pallid version it was monotonous and low-pitched. Finally, the originators of the exemplars were either the interviewed persons themselves or their paraphrased equivalent as articulated by the reporters. The originator variation was applied because it was assumed that original interviews are more vivid than the reporters' summaries (cf. Gibson & Zillmann, 1993, 1998).

Preliminary analyses examined the perception of the stories across different experimental conditions. Perceived credibility, vividness, and origination were of particular interest. Regarding credibility, three of the four stories (the apple wine story being the exception) showed it to be somewhat higher for base-rate-consistent than for base-rate-inconsistent exemplification. However, the difference did not exceed a scale point, and the ratings of the less credible condition were above the midpoint of the 7-point scale. Credibility thus may be considered to have been at average levels. Regarding the vividness manipulations, all four stories featuring original interviews were perceived as being more vivid than their counterparts with paraphrased summaries. Similarly, all four stories featuring vivid language were perceived as being more vivid than their counterparts with pallid language. Both manipulations of vividness thus may be considered to have been successful.

The analysis of the first focal measure, the perception of public opinion, yielded highly significant results for exemplification. As can be seen from Table 4.2, the effects were consistent across all stories. Perceived majority and minority opinions followed the ratio of the exemplar distributions. In the first story, for instance, the base-rate information indicated that the large majority of citizens opposed card telephones. With consistency between base rates and exemplification, the perceived distribution of opinions reflected the distribution of exemplars rather closely: four against and one in favor of card telephones. In the case of incompatibility between base rates and exemplification, the perception of majority and minority opinions was also guided by the exemplar distribution—this despite the fact that the base-rate information clearly indicated majority opinion to the contrary. This outcome lends considerable evidence to the proposal that the aggregation of exemplars influences the perception of public opinion on social issues more strongly than general, abstract statements. Although the base-rate information was explicit and unambiguous, recipients apparently paid little attention to it and judged the issue in accordance with the distribution of exemplars.

The originator and language-vividness manipulations exerted minor and no influence, respectively. An effect favoring interviews over paraphrasing was observed for the apple wine story but not for any of the other stories. Interactions between origination and exemplification suggest that the presentation of interviews

TABLE 4.2
Percentage Estimates of Public Opinion as a Function
of Relative Frequency of Exemplification in Radio News Reports

| Report Issue | Base Rate | Exemplification Relative to Base Rate | |
| --- | --- | --- | --- |
| | | Consistent | Inconsistent |
| Card telephone | Majority | 77.6[a] | 34.0[b] |
| Cafeteria food | Minority | 21.1[b] | 58.9[a] |
| Apple wine | Minority | 21.8[b] | 73.4[a] |
| PC courses | Majority | 78.6[a] | 24.7[b] |

*Note.* The exemplar ratio was 4:1 for consistent and 1:4 for inconsistent exemplification. Means having different superscripts differ significantly at $p < .05$. Comparisons are within stories only. Authors' data, first published in "The utility of exemplars in persuasive communications," by H.-B. Brosius and A. Bathelt, 1994, *Communication Research, 21*(1), 48–78.

TABLE 4.3

Percentage Estimates of Personal Opinion as a Function
of Relative Frequency of Exemplification in Radio News Reports

| | | Exemplification Relative to Base Rate | |
|---|---|---|---|
| Report Issue | Base Rate | Consistent | Inconsistent |
| Card telephone | Majority | 62.0[a] | 53.1[b] |
| Cafeteria food | Minority | 29.4[b] | 43.3[a] |
| Apple wine | Minority | 48.1[b] | 57.2[a] |
| PC courses | Majority | 55.5[a] | 42.5[b] |

*Note.* Legend of Table 4.2 applies.

amplified the effect of exemplification in three of the four stories (card telephones, cafeteria food, and apple wine). The more vivid presentation using interviews enlarged the difference between consistent and inconsistent exemplification.

The analysis of the second focal measure, personal opinion, also yielded significant results for exemplification. The exemplar distributions influenced the respondents' own opinions on all presented issues. Independent of base-rate information, they tended to follow the majority opinion suggested by the distribution of exemplars. Table 4.3 summarizes these findings.

The second experiment was conducted as a follow-up on the first in order to examine once more the vivid-language effect that had proved elusive. A factorial design was employed, varying only the distribution of exemplars (consistent or inconsistent with base rates) and their language vividness (vivid or pallid). The exemplars were presented as original interviews. In contrast to the first experiment, base rates were formulated in relative, vague terms. The anchor spoke about "more and more people" or an "increasing number of people" who, for instance, liked or disliked the university's cafeteria food. Such suggestive, relative base rates do not reveal the actual number or proportion of people involved. They may be interpreted, nonetheless, as indicating the involvement of "a great many people," if not "nearly everybody"—this despite the possibility that the statement may concerns changes within a small minority (cf. Brosius, Breinker, & Esser, 1991).

A strong effect of exemplification on the perception of public opinion was again observed for all four stories. The associated means are displayed in Table 4.4. As can be seen, the findings fully replicate those of the first experiment. The perception of majority and of minority opinions again followed the exemplar distributions, and any influence of base-rate information was negligible. Vividness of language failed once more, however, to exert appreciable effects. The findings concerning the respondents' personal opinions, finally, were weaker than in the prior experiment. Although the mean differentiation suggested the expected effects of exemplar distributions, the effect was significant only for the cafeteria food story. This lack of overall differentiation may be the result of diminished statistical power,

TABLE 4.4
Replication of Percentage Estimates of Public Opinion as a Function
of Relative Frequency of Exemplification in Radio News Reports

| Report Issue | Base Rate | Exemplification Relative to Base Rate | |
| --- | --- | --- | --- |
| | | Consistent | Inconsistent |
| Card telephone | Majority | 83.2[a] | 27.0[b] |
| Cafeteria food | Minority | 15.6[b] | 75.4[a] |
| Apple wine | Minority | 18.8[b] | 77.5[a] |
| PC courses | Majority | 78.9[a] | 16.2[b] |

Note. Legend of Table 4.2 applies.

as the number of respondents in the second experiment was less than half of that in the first.

The third experiment examined the effects of different ratios of exemplar to counterexemplar distributions. Specifically, several such distributions were ordered in terms of apparent majority or minority dominance in order to determine the consequences of these exemplification impressions.

The vague base-rate presentation of the second experiment was retained, but only the vivid interviews were employed (i.e., their comparison with reporter summaries was omitted). The design varied the correspondence between exemplar distributions and base rates (consistent or inconsistent) with six exemplification ratios: 4:0, 4:1, 3:1, 2:0, 2:2, and 1:1. Thus, when the base-rate information indicated, for instance, that more and more students were dissatisfied with the university's cafeteria food, in the 3:1 consistent condition the reporter interviewed three students who disliked the food and one student who liked it. In the 1:3 inconsistent condition, the ratio was reversed, yielding interviews with three students who liked the food and one student who disliked it.

Exemplar distributions consequently varied between the extremes of being entirely consistent with base-rate information (4:0 ratio) to being completely contradictory to it (0:4 ratio). An ordering of these ratios was accomplished by simply computing the difference between the number of consistent and inconsistent exemplars for each ratio. These differences, varying from +4 to −4, defined the exemplification variable that was used in regression analyses of the ordered ratios. The focal measures were, of course, the perception of public opinion and the respondents' personal views.

Figure 4.1 shows that, irrespective of base rate information (which was identical in all conditions), the distribution of perceived public opinion very closely followed the distribution of majority-projecting exemplification. The indicated linear relationship proved to be highly significant for all stories employed (i.e., for card telephones, cafeteria food, apple wine, and PC courses). Ignoring contradictory base-rate information, respondents who were exposed to just four exemplars

## Perception of Other's Wine Evaluation

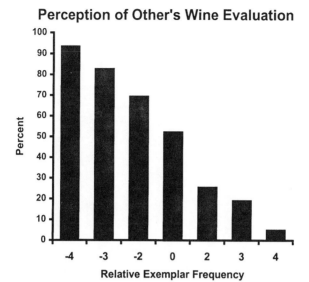

FIG. 4.1  Perception of Other's Evaluation of the quality of local apple wine as a function of radio news alleging that a decreasing number of people like the wine (base rate) and various interviews with wine drinkers whose statements were either consistent or inconsistent with this projection. Minus 4 indicates that four interviewees are reported to like the wine; plus 4 indicates that four interviewees reported to dislike it. The other conditions involved countercontentions. Minus 3 (1:4) indicates one countercontention; plus 3 indicates the same ratio, but in reverse (4:1). Minus 2 combines two conditions (1:3 and 0:2), with plus 2 again indicating inversion (3:1 and 2:0). Zero also combines two conditions (2:2 and 1:1). Authors' data, first published in "The utility of exemplars in persuasive communications," by H.-B. Brosius and A. Bathelt, 1994, *Communication Research, 21*(1), 48–78.

of interviewees claiming to like the cafeteria food, for instance, projected this ratio onto the population—actually approximating the extreme of 100%. Being exposed to merely four interviewees claiming to detest the food produced similarly extreme results, with respondents apparently believing that hardly anybody would like it. It is also surprising that, despite base-rate information to the contrary, respondents based population projections of approximately 50% on exemplar–counterexemplar matches of only two cases, even only one case, on each side.

The extreme differentiation observed for the perception of public opinion did not extend to personal opinions. Figure 4.2 shows the effect of the exemplification variation on the respondents' personal views. The linear relationship from +4 to −4 exemplification was comparatively poor. It was significant only for the cafeteria food and the apple wine stories (the effect for the latter story being shown in the

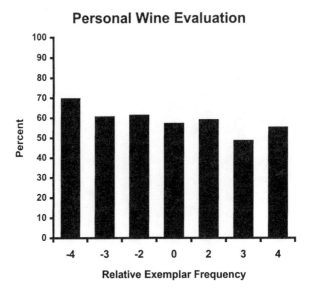

FIG. 4.2    Personal Evaluation of the quality of local apple wine as a
function of radio news alleging that a decreasing number of people
like the wine (base rate) and various interviews with wine drinkers
whose estimates were either consistent or inconsistent with this projection. The conditions are detailed in the legend to Fig. 4.1. Authors'
data, first published in "The utility of exemplars in persuasive communications," by H.-B. Brosius and A. Bathelt, 1994, *Communication
Research, 21*(1), 48–78.

figure), and it merely approached significance for the card telephone and the PC
course stories. Still, the findings support the contention that personal opinion
tends to reflect the dominant position exhibited in the aggregation of exemplars
and counterexemplars.

The fourth experiment was designed to extend the reported effects from radio-
news to print-news presentations and to explore the duration of exemplification
influence. Medium of presentation (radio vs. newspaper), exemplar distribution
relative to base rate (consistent vs. inconsistent), and time of measurement (immediately vs. 1 week after exposure) were factorially varied. Base-rate information
was again relative and vague. Exemplars were vividly phrased and presented in the
initially used ratio of 4:1. However, in the interest of ecological validity, the print
version displayed the exemplars in the form of a reporter summary. Additionally,
this experiment addressed solely the perception of public opinion.

The findings concerning estimates of the distribution of public opinion that
were made immediately after exposure to the news are summarized in Table 4.5.
As can be seen, the repeatedly observed exemplification effects are again in evidence. These effects manifested themselves in response to print news almost as

TABLE 4.5
Post-Exposure Percentage Estimates of Public Opinion as a Function
of Relative Frequency of Exemplification in Radio and in Print-News Reports

| | | Radio | | Print | |
| --- | --- | --- | --- | --- | --- |
| | | Exemplification Relative to Base Rate | | | |
| Report Issue | Base Rate | Consistent | Inconsistent | Consistent | Inconsistent |
| Card telephone | Majority | 78.2[a] | 20.0[b] | 75.8[a] | 26.2[b] |
| Cafeteria food | Minority | 19.1[b] | 61.8[a] | 15.8[a] | 64.2[b] |
| Apple wine | Minority | 16.1[b] | 77.2[a] | 23.2[a] | 72.6[b] |
| PC courses | Majority | 78.6[a] | 18.6[b] | 77.3[a] | 23.5[b] |

Note. Legend of Table 4.2 applies.

TABLE 4.6
One-Week Delayed Percentage Estimates of Public Opinion as a Function
of Relative Frequency of Exemplification in Radio and in Print-News Reports

| | | Radio | | Print | |
| --- | --- | --- | --- | --- | --- |
| | | Exemplification Relative to Base Rate | | | |
| Report Issue | Base Rate | Consistent | Inconsistent | Consistent | Inconsistent |
| Card telephone | Majority | 72.2[a] | 45.1[b] | 74.7[a] | 46.7[b] |
| Cafeteria food | Minority | 23.7[b] | 52.9[a] | 25.3[a] | 45.0[b] |
| Apple wine | Minority | 24.6[b] | 68.2[a] | 36.6[a] | 57.6[b] |
| PC courses | Majority | 61.4[a] | 33.3[b] | 59.1[a] | 42.6[b] |

Note. Legend of Table 4.2 applies.

strongly as in response to the same news presented by radio. The minor medium difference may actually result from the loss of a degree of vividness due to using reporter summaries in the print mode. On the whole, however, the findings show the effects of exemplification to be medium-independent. By demonstrating immediate effects of print-news, they also extend the findings reported by Zillmann and associates (1992) that are summarized in Table 4.1.

The findings concerning the public-opinion estimates made 1 week after exposure to the news are summarized in Table 4.6. These findings, as can be seen, show the persistence of the exemplification effects over the time period in question, and they show this for both media, radio and print. Over time, the differentiation of consistent and inconsistent exemplification grew somewhat weaker, however. For radio news, the difference across all four stories averaged 56% immediately after exposure. After 1 week's time, this difference was 32%, the reduction amounting to 24%. For print news, this decline in differentiation was 29% (50% immediately after exposure, 21% after the delay). The change over time in the perception of public opinion is interesting in yet another way. It will be recalled that in the investigation by Zillmann and associates (1992) estimates of the incidence of weight regainers had regressed toward earlier held beliefs within 2 weeks. As earlier beliefs are not an issue with the topics addressed in the stories used by Brosius (1995), it may be expected, as some uncertainty must have set in with time, that judgments regressed toward guessing—that is, toward 50% estimates. This was indeed the case. The absolute value of the discrepancy of estimates from 50% was computed and averaged across the four stories. Regarding radio news, the averages for consistent exemplification fell from 30% to 21%. Likewise, they fell from 25% to 11% for inconsistent exemplification. The corresponding changes for print news were from 28% to 18% for inconsistent exemplification and from 22% to 6% for consistent exemplification. The discrepancy from 50% thus diminished consistently over time. Such regressive changes may be expected to continue and to eventually remove the effects of exemplification. It remains unclear, however, at which time the indicated effect dissipation may be complete. The findings of the reported experiment show that the exemplification effect changed only trivially in one week's time. It can only be conjectured how many more weeks it may have persisted. What has been demonstrated compellingly is that the effects under consideration are not limited to minutes, to hours, or to days, but may persist for truly extended periods of time.

The fifth experiment was conducted to determine whether or not the consistently negligible effect of base-rate information resulted from the early placement of that information, giving a recency advantage to the subsequently placed exemplars. This advantage was removed be repeating the base rate at the end of the report. This way, base-rate information was favored not only by primacy and by recency but also was presented twice. Furthermore, in order to strengthen the base rate's valence in its informational competition with associated exemplars, the argumentation by interviewees was weakened in one condition. In a pretest, respondents rated the persuasive strength of all exemplars used in the previous experiments. For each story the weakest argument was identified, and four variants of this argument were created. These poor and redundant arguments then were used in the condition featuring weak argumentation. In the strong argumentation condition, recipients were exposed to four different, stronger arguments. The design thus varied exemplar distribution (consistent vs. inconsistent), repetition of the base-rate information (yes vs. no), and strength of arguments (strong vs. weak). The exemplar distribution was either 4:1 or 1:4 as in the preceding experiment. The experiment was conducted with print news.

The findings are presented in Tables 4.7 and 4.8. As can be seen, neither the repetition of base-rate information nor the weakening of exemplar argumentation appreciably altered the dominant influence of consistent and of inconsistent exemplar distributions over base rates.

Independent of exemplification, however, both the repetition of base-rate information and the strength of exemplar argumentation exerted minor effects on

TABLE 4.7
Percentage Estimates of Public Opinion as a Function of Relative Frequency of
Exemplification and of Base-Rate Repetition in Print-News Reports

| | | Base-Rate Presentation | | | |
| | | At Outset Only | | At Outset and End | |
| | | Exemplification Relative to Base Rate | | | |
| Report Issue | Base Rate | Consistent | Inconsistent | Consistent | Inconsistent |
|---|---|---|---|---|---|
| Card telephone | Majority | 66.5[a] | 38.8[b] | 68.8[a] | 40.2[b] |
| Cafeteria food | Minority | 30.3[b] | 58.7[a] | 23.7[a] | 50.1[b] |
| Apple wine | Minority | 41.0[b] | 69.5[a] | 36.3[a] | 61.6[b] |
| PC courses | Majority | 69.8[a] | 38.7[b] | 65.2[a] | 42.4[b] |

*Note.* Legend of Table 4.2 applies.


TABLE 4.8
Percentage Estimates of Public Opinion as a Function of Relative Frequency
of Exemplification and of Argument Strength in Print-News Reports

| | | Exemplar Arguments | | | |
| | | Strong | | Weak | |
| | | Exemplification Relative to Base Rate | | | |
| Report Issue | Base Rate | Consistent | Inconsistent | Consistent | Inconsistent |
|---|---|---|---|---|---|
| Card telephone | Majority | 66.1[a] | 34.5[b] | 69.2[a] | 44.7[b] |
| Cafeteria food | Minority | 32.8[b] | 56.8[a] | 21.0[a] | 52.0[b] |
| Apple wine | Minority | 44.6[b] | 68.6[a] | 32.6[a] | 62.6[b] |
| PC courses | Majority | 66.8[a] | 36.4[b] | 68.2[a] | 44.6[b] |

*Note.* Legend of Table 4.2 applies.


estimates. Regarding base-rate repetition, only the cafeteria food story yielded a significant main effect. After only one presentation of the minority-projecting base rate, estimates were at 44%; after repeated presentation they dropped to 37% (i.e., they became more indicative of a minority). Regarding argumentation strength, the main effect was significant for three of the four stories, and it approached significance for the fourth story (PC courses). In the minority-projecting base-rate cases, poor argumentation reduced estimates, as expected (i.e., they allowed base rates to exert relatively greater influence). In case of the cafeteria-food story, estimates for weak argumentation were at 36%, as compared to strong argumentation at 45%. In the parallel case of the cafeteria food story, estimates for weak argumentation were at 48%, as compared to strong argumentation at 57%. Also as expected, poor argumentation increased estimates in the majority-projecting base-rate case of the card-telephone story. Estimates for weak argumentation were at 57%, as compared to strong argumentation at 50%.

The results of the fifth experiment thus indicate that the repetition of base-rate information, and somewhat more so the weakening of arguments in exemplars, may exert a degree of influence on the perception of public opinion, essentially strengthening the effect of base-rate information. However, the reported findings show these effects to be minor and incapable of removing the far stronger effects of exemplification.

The sixth and final investigation in this series examined the effects of affinity between persons presented in exemplars and news recipients. Specifically, the experiment was designed to determine whether or not the respondents' perception of similarity between themselves and person exemplars—similarity in terms of demographic characteristics, for instance—would increase the effectiveness of exemplification.

Analogous to the preceding experiments, four stories were presented. In all cases, the base-rate information, displayed at the outset as well as in the heading, defined the majority opinion by usage of phrases like "A clear majority . . . ," or "Most. . . ." This text did not indicate percentages in order to prevent binding recall of exact ratios. Five exemplars were featured. In them, persons expressed distinct opinions concerning the addressed issue. The ratio of favoring versus opposing a particular position was 4:1 or 1:4, respectively. The exemplar distribution thus was either consistent or inconsistent with the heading and the reporter's summary. In the articles, exemplars with a high degree of similarity to the student recipients were described as "students." Exemplars with a low degree of similarity to the student recipients were described as "retirees." Portraits of students and retirees were used to create conspicuous exemplars. The portraits were omitted in a relatively pallid countercondition. The design thus varied the distribution of exemplars, group membership, and illustration. More specifically, it varied exemplars relative to base-rate information (representative vs. discrepant), the social group of the exemplars (students vs. retirees), and illustration (portraits present vs. absent).

The four stories were printed in the style of newspaper articles. The text of the introductory base-rate information was identical in all conditions. Persons shown or cited as exemplars were identified as students or as retirees by providing for each a fictitious name, age, and occupation. An opinion was attributed, for instance, to "Tanja Sievers (22), student of psychology." Appropriate portraits were taken from existing collections. Photographs showing young adults, apparently aged 20 to 30 years, were selected as student portraits. Photographs showing older adults, apparently aged 60 to 70 years, were selected were as portraits of retirees. The story on the quality on university cafeteria food obviously did not lend itself to being used with the retirees. It was consequently replaced by the aforementioned story about a plan for the creation of a traffic-free pedestrian zone. In this story, the base-rate information projected a majority opposition to the plan.

Results are in terms of the focal measures of the perception of public opinion and of personal preference. The analysis of the effects of exemplification on public opinion again yielded significant findings for all four stories. The card telephone story related that the vast majority of citizens opposed their introduction. Four interviews with citizens opposing the phones fostered a majority perception at 61%. Four interviews with citizens taking a stand in favor of the phones, despite base rates to the contrary, reduced this perception to 49%. Similarly, when the persons quoted came out against the banning of traffic from the inner city, which corresponded with the base-rate information, respondents thought that 54% of the citizens were against the traffic ban; when the quoted persons were in favor of the ban, only 47% were opposed to it. When the exemplars favored tele-shopping (again corresponding with base rates), respondents believed that 40% were supportive; when the exemplars opposed tele-shopping, only 34% were supportive. Finally, when the exemplified persons judged the apple wine to be of poor quality (which, according to the base-rate information, was the majority opinion), respondents thought that 40% of the citizenry considered the wine quality to be poor; when the exemplified persons judged the wine to be excellent, only 22% considered its quality poor. All of these differences were highly significant and thus corroborate the findings of the earlier experiments. However, compared with the results of these earlier experiments, the differences between base-rate consistent and base-rate inconsistent exemplar distributions were notably smaller. For instance, in the fourth experiment averages of 76% (consistent) and 26% (inconsistent) were observed for the card telephone issue. The corresponding difference in the sixth experiment is only that between 61% and 49%. A partial explanation for this discrepancy is that the base-rate information was given twice, once obtrusively in the heading and once in the lead of the article (whereas in the earlier experiment it was given only in the lead). This difference in base-rate presentation might account for the change from 26% to 49% in the condition where the base-rate information is challenged by the exemplars.

The respondents' personal opinion was affected by the distribution of exemplars in only one of the four issues: the quality of apple wine, or rather the lack thereof. Respondents exposed to a majority of exemplars alleging the wine's poor quality, along with corresponding base-rate information, judged the wine to be of poorer quality than did their counterparts who had been exposed to four persons who thought the wine to be excellent. On a bad–good scale ranging from one to nine, the former group gave the wine an average rating of 3.8; the latter gave it, on average, a 5.1 rating. Considering earlier observations also, it appears that exemplification exerts its strongest influence on personal opinion when evaluations are a matter of taste.

The degree of affinity between exemplified persons and recipients, operationalized in age differences, and the format of exemplar presentation, operationalized by absence versus presence of portraits, failed to yield appreciable effects on either one of the focal measures—the perception of public and personal opinion. This failure is the likely result of a lack of salience of age differences between the persons who expressed their views concerning the issues of the four stories. None of the issues is particularly age specific, making the testimony of young persons and of old persons equally relevant. The outcome might have been different, for instance, had the preference for adolescent music been at issue. As it stands, however, public phones are used by students and by retirees; the traffic ban and tele-shopping concern both groups; and apple wine is a favorite among the young and the old. Given the absence of differential salience, the portraits could only underscore a nonpertinent age discrepancy. The findings, then, suggest that the recipients' siding with similar exemplified others is by no means automatic and seems to depend on the sharing of features that are salient yet distinct along the similarity–dissimilarity continuum.

Zillmann, Gibson, Sundar, and Perkins (1996) extended the earlier research on the interplay of influence exerted over time by base-rate information and by exemplification (Zillmann et al., 1992). Specifically, these investigators selected an issue for which prior knowledge was negligible, if at all existent. In the earlier research, as might be recalled, 2 weeks after exposure to a news report on weight regaining the respondents returned to initially held beliefs. The new topic, the economics of family farming, was expected to prevent such regression, as specific prior beliefs were not established. A further extension was the involvement of a secondary issue concomitant with the primary one.

A story entitled "Banks and Farmers Plowing Same Ground for Cash Crops" addressed the financial woes of American family farmers, largely blaming greedy bankers for the farmers' problems. The report was presented as a page from *U.S. News & World Report*. It was paged, dated, and attributed to two correspondents. The report's manipulation was analogous to that of the earlier investigation on weight regaining.

Base-rate information was either precise or vague. Its manipulation was as follows—with the text in single brackets indicating precise base rates, and that in double brackets indicating vague base rates.

> [Nearly one out of every three family farms] [[A lot of the farms]] in America lose money, according to a study by a consortium of Midwestern universities. "The country's farmers are losing [some $50 million a year] [[millions each year]]," says J. Patrick Irons, director of the U.S. Agrarian Research Institute in Chicago, Ill., which funded the study. [In 70 percent of the cases] [[Much of the time]], the study determined, banks were largely responsible for the farmers' financial woes.

The exemplars featured either farmers in financial difficulties or financially successful farmers. These farmers either blamed the banks for their problems or praised them for their good fortunes. Exemplars were as follows.

Farmer in difficulties:

> Josh Davidson of Waterloo, Iowa, wiped the grease off his calloused hands after replacing the ball bearings on a 15-year-old combine he bought from a neighbor. After

losing money for the fifth year in a row, Davidson had to sell his new equipment, lay off most of his hired help and take a winter job working for the state.

"I'd quit farming, but I refuse to allow the bank to gain control of my farm," he says. "Bank officials begged me to borrow more money to finance more acreage and more equipment. 'You're a good farmer; you can make it big, Josh.' Now look at me — farming more acres with fewer hired men and older equipment while interest payments suck out every cent of profit and more."

Successful farmer:

During the bad years, the banks continued to offer William Moore of Carrolton, Texas, loans, and now he's making more money in one year than he did in the first five of the 1980s. Moore's farm belonged first to his grandfather, and the third generation owner refused to cut back on his acreage even though it has required greater overhead and debt.

"I've always considered myself a conservative businessman," Moore says. "I haven't bought bigger equipment, and now I'm less dependent upon the bank to stay in business and I'm making money to pay back loans. Sometimes I wonder if that's exactly what the financial institution had in mind when it believed in me enough to loan me money in the first place."

In a condition of *selective exemplification,* nine exemplars of farmers in financial difficulty were aggregated. This aggregation corresponds with the so-called slant of the story. In a condition of *representative exemplification,* the distribution followed the precise base-rate information. The one-third minority of failing farms was represented by three exemplars and the two-third majority of solvent and successful farms was represented by six exemplars. This ratio was reversed to create a condition of *blended exemplification.*

The procedure employed was that of the earlier investigation. Respondents read three stories, but shortly after reading them they were tested only on two of the issues addressed. The issue of one story was skipped to allow for delayed testing. Respondents in the immediate-effects condition indicated their perceptions concerning the farming issue shortly after reading about it. Respondents in the delayed-effects condition were initially tested on unrelated issues and only after a 2-week delay indicated their perceptions concerning the farming issue.

The findings are summarized in Table 4.9. As can be seen, the prevalence of failing farms was grossly overestimated after exposure to selective exemplification. Following a highly significant linear trend, overestimation diminished toward representative exemplification, with the compromise exemplar distribution assuming an intermediate position.

Not shown in the table is the fact that the estimates were retained over time. That is, estimates obtained after a 2-week delay did not appreciably differ from those attained shortly after story exposure. Technically speaking, there was no indication of a main effect of time after exposure or of an interaction of the time variable with exemplification. In the absence of firmly established prior beliefs,

TABLE 4.9

Initial Experiment on Farming: Estimates of the Incidence of Failing Family Farms and of Bankers' Responsibility as a Function of Exemplification

| | Exemplification | | |
|---|---|---|---|
| Measures | Selective | Blended | Representative |
| Failing farms | 68.85[a] | 60.87[b] | 54.00[c] |
| Bankers' fault | 59.00[a] | 47.02[b] | 46.96[b] |

Note. Estimates are in percent. Means associated with different letter superscripts differ significantly at $p < .05$. Comparisons are within measures only. Authors' data, first published in "Effects of exemplification in news reports on the perception of social issues," by D. Zillmann, R. Gibson, S. S. Sundar, and J. W. Perkins, 1996, Journalism and Mass Communication Quarterly, 73(2), 427–444.

then, the effects created by different exemplar distributions were stable over time, enduring at least a 2-week period.

The complete absence of base-rate effects is also not shown in the table. The verbal presentation of a precise ratio (i.e., one third) may have been especially unobtrusive and therefore readily overlooked.

As expected, the concomitant variation of the bankers' culpability yielded essentially parallel effects. Selective exemplification not only fostered exaggerated estimates of failing farms but also prompted the strongest indictment of the bankers.

The bankers' culpability had been assessed on a percentage scale that ascribed complementary fault to farmers (e.g., if bankers' fault relative to that of farmers was 90%, the farmers took the blame for 10%). In order to remove this constraint and allow the independent assessment of the bankers' versus the farmers' fault for the failing of farms, more appropriate scales were created, and the experiment was replicated. The only other modification concerns the time delay. It was 1 week, instead of 2 weeks.

The findings, summarized in Table 4.10, fully replicate those of the preceding investigation. Exemplification produced the same highly significant trend from gross overestimation of the incidence of failing farms in the selective-exemplification condition to the least inaccurate estimation in the representative-exemplification condition. This effect was again stable over time. There was no indication of an interaction between time and exemplification or of a main effect of time. Moreover, base-rate information again was entirely inconsequential.

The apportionment of blame for the farmers' financial woes was as expected. Selective exemplification resulted in ascriptions of much culpability to the bankers and minimal fault to the farmers. The assignment of blame was markedly less polarized in the conditions of blended and of representative exemplification.

The investigation also ascertained the respondents' emotional reactions to the news report. Selective exemplification, featuring nine farmers in financial difficul-

TABLE 4.10
Replication Experiment on Farming:
Estimates of the Incidence of Failing Family Farms and Ratings
of Bankers' Versus Farmers' Fault as a Function of Exemplification

| | Exemplification | | |
|---|---|---|---|
| Measures | Selective | Blended | Representative |
| Failing farms | 65.92[a] | 55.67[b] | 52.71[b] |
| Bankers' fault | 6.88[a] | 5.77[b] | 5.32[b] |
| Farmers' fault | 3.10[b] | 4.08[a] | 4.47[a] |

*Note.* Estimates of failing farms are in percent. Ratings are on scales ranging from zero to 10. Means associated with different letter superscripts differ significantly at $p < .05$. Comparisons are within measures only. Authors' data, first published in "Effects of exemplification in news reports on the perception of social issues," by D. Zillmann, R. Gibson, S. S. Sundar, and J. W. Perkins, 1996, *Journalism and Mass Communication Quarterly, 73*(2), 427–444.

ties who lamented their plight and blamed it on irresponsible bankers, proved to be more distressing than the other exemplifications. Respondents reported, for instance, having been more upset while reading and worrying more about the issue.

An investigation by Daschmann (1999) extended the research on exemplar effects to political communication—to newspaper reports of forthcoming elections and their anticipated outcome in particular.

Base-rate information was provided with the poll-based projection of either an incumbent party-coalition's election victory or defeat. In a control condition, the election outcome was not forecast. These three conditions were cross-varied with exemplar additions that featured either dominantly antigovernment interviews (four anti vs. one pro) or dominantly progovernment interviews (four pro vs. one anti). A control condition did not present interviews. The exemplars presented potential voters who gave reasons for voting for or against the coalition in power. They did not indicate their voting intentions, however. The design thus was a 3 × 3 factorial one, with base-rate information (projection of defeat, no projection, projection of victory) and exemplification (antigovernmental, none, progovernmental) as factors. The dependent measures were opinions about voting in terms of progovernmental support and election victory, opinions about the government's past performance, and the respondents' own voting intentions.

The exemplar variation produced strong effects on both voting measures. The effects are summarized in Fig. 4.3. Compared against the control, as can be seen, dominantly antigovernmental exemplification reduced voting and victory estimates, whereas dominantly progovernmental exemplification increased these estimates. All indicated exemplification effects were highly significant.

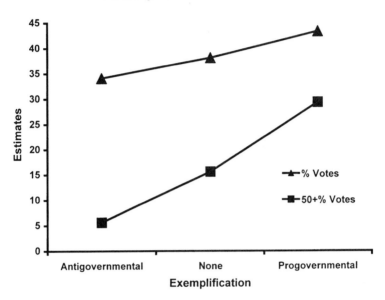

FIG. 4.3    Exemplification effects in political communication. The estimates are of progovernmental voting. Percent estimates are in mean scores. Victory estimates (i.e., 50+%
estimates of an absolute majority) are in frequencies. From *Vox pop & polls: The impact of
poll results and voter statements on voter judgment,* by G. Daschmann, 1999 (May), paper
presented to the Political Communication Division at the Annual Conference of the International Communication Association, San Francisco, CA. Adapted with permission.

On the measure of progovernmental voting, the base-rate information yielded
a significant main effect also. Victory projection (41.2%) fostered higher estimates
than defeat projection (35.8%). These estimates did not appreciably differ from
the control (38.3%), however. As there were no interactions in the analysis of this
measure, the base-rate effect proved to be independent of the exemplification
effect. On the measure of victory estimates (i.e., of absolute majority estimates),
the findings paralleled those of the voting-percentage estimates. The differentiation proved negligible, however. Taken together, then, the perception of likely
voting by the constituency was strongly influenced by exemplification. Moreover,
this exemplification effect was markedly stronger and more robust than the effect
of base-rate information. Once again, respondents based their assessments, first
and foremost, on concrete yet fickle exemplifying testimony of people rather than
on more reliable abstract information.

The evaluation of the incumbent government's past performance largely followed the described pattern. The differentiation was less pronounced, however.
With ratings ranging from zero (very bad) to 100 (very good), progovernmental

exemplification (56.0) led to more favorable evaluations than did antigovernmental exemplification (49.0). Evaluations in the control were intermediate (52.6) and were not appreciably different from those in the exemplar conditions. The base-rate variation proved inconsequential for this evaluation.

The exemplification effects on voting by the constituency and on the evaluation of the government's performance did not translate to voting intentions. The nonparametric analysis of this measure did not yield significant results.

In summary, the following conclusions may be drawn from this research on the effects of different distributions of exemplars and counterexemplars.

1. The ratio of exemplars to counterexemplars of specific occurrences consistently exerts a dominant influence on the perception of these occurrences in the population under consideration. Exemplification of opinions and preferences, for instance, largely determines a corresponding perception of public opinion and preferences of the public.

2. Exemplar–counterexemplar ratios that correctly represent the population distribution of occurrences foster comparatively correct population estimates. Selective, entirely focus-driven exemplification fosters the least correct population estimates. Intermediate, blended distributions produce intermediate results. Representative exemplification of opinions and preferences thus may be expected to yield the most correct perception of public opinion and preferences of the public. Selective exemplification, in contrast, must be expected to yield the most distorted, incorrect perceptions.

3. The ratio of exemplars to counterexemplars exerts some degree of influence on personal opinion and preference. This influence is less consistent and generally less strong, however. It appears to be partial to judgments concerning taste, such as those concerning food preference.

4. The effects specified in (1) through (3) are medium-independent, as they apply to both print and radio presentations.

5. The indicated effects, especially those specified in (1) and (2), may persist for extended periods of time, such as over 2 weeks and potentially much longer. Enduring effects may be expected in situations where prior beliefs about the addressed issue are vague or nonexistent. In situations where prior beliefs are firmly established, effects are likely to be short-lived.

6. Base-rate information, whether precise or vague, has minor, if any, effects on the perception of public opinion or on preferences of the public. Its influence is generally overpowered by that of exemplar aggregation. The within-text display of base-rate information is mostly inconsequential. There is indication, however, that base-rate repetition and concluding placement can give this information some degree of influence. Additionally, diminishing the persuasive strength of exemplars may enhance the relative influence of base-rate information.

7. Affinity between exemplified persons and recipients does not, in and of itself, enhance the effects of exemplification. Specifically, if similarity–dissimilarity

does not covary with distinct appraisals of an addressed phenomenon, the degree of affinity appears to be without consequence for the perception of public opinion and preferences of the public.

8. Given the conditions specified in (7), the pictorial presentation of persons in exemplars does not appear to enhance the effects of exemplification.

## Base-Rate Influence

The generalization that the influence of base-rate information is largely compromised by that of exemplification has not gone unchallenged. Some of the experiments reported by Brosius and Bathelt (1994), as will be recalled, already involved manipulations that were expected to enhance the effect of base-rate presentation. In the first experiment of their series, they attempted to weaken the competing exemplar information by use of pallid language and by summarizing. The second experiment similarly featured pallid language of exemplars in one condition. The fifth experiment weakened the argument strength of exemplars and, more important, repeated the base-rate information obtrusively at the end of the news report. All of these variations bore little result.

Two experiments have gone further, however, in creating conditions that give the influence advantage to base-rate information over exemplars, actually over a singular exemplar.

Baesler and Burgoon (1994) exposed respondents to a written report on juvenile delinquency and measured their perceptions concerning issue and report at different times after exposure (immediately, after a 2-day delay, and after a delay of 1 week). The report manipulation was twofold, with story versus statistics being crossvaried with vivid versus nonvivid language. The message opened with general arguments concerning juvenile delinquency and then featured either a story about an individual or statistical information. The story related scenes, characters, conflict, and resolution of the singular case. The base-rate alternative provided relevant numeric information, such as percentages and odds, about several hundred adolescents. The statistics were emphasized by underlining them. "This form of statistical presentation was used to compensate for the underutilization of statistics in previous research (Nisbett, Krantz, Jepson, & Kunda, 1983)" (Baesler & Burgoon, 1994, p. 588). The report's persuasiveness was ascertained in the agreement with statements such as "Juvenile delinquents grow up to become criminals."

The findings revealed that the statistics-laden report was more persuasive than the report presenting a singular exemplar. The other variables failed to exert reliable influence. The absence of a main effect of time of measurement and an interaction between time and story versus statistics indicates that the differential persuasiveness of story and statistics was retained over time. This finding lends further evidence to the endurance of base-rate and exemplification effects (cf. Zillmann et al., 1996; also Experiment 4 of Brosius & Bathelt, 1994). The failure of obtaining meaningful effects of vividness variations is also consistent with earlier observations (Brosius & Bathelt, 1994).

The findings presented by Baesler and Burgoon (1994) establish, no doubt, that conditions exist under which the influence of base-rate information overwhelms that of exemplars. They suggest that, if base rates are emphasized to a point where recipients must pay attention to them, they are bound to exert their influence, especially when informational competition from exemplars is poor—such as in a one-exemplar case.

An investigation by Krupat, Smith, Leach, and Jackson (1997) extended this attentional-focus rationale of base-rate influence to include the base rates' diagnostic relevance. These investigators exposed respondents to an essay about a fictitious new car, the Clipper, said to be imported from Denmark. The essay either related the findings of a survey of 1,000 owners, according to which the Clipper suffered from numerous mechanical problems (base-rate condition), or it recounted a single family's problems with the car, culminating in its stalling once on a railroad track (exemplar condition). Following the one or the other essay was an editorial note that alleged misrepresentation and enumerated the car's qualities either in story (i.e., exemplar) or in statistical (i.e., base rate) fashion. Specifically, the base-rate essay was followed by a corrective note expressed in exemplar form, whereas the exemplar essay was followed by a corrective note in base-rate terms. Respondents rated the desirability of the fictitious car either after reading the first essay only or after reading this essay followed by the editorial note with opposing claims.

Exposure to the base-rate and the exemplar essays prompted similar assessments. Additionally, the provision of statistical information first, followed by that of an opposing exemplar in the editorial note, did not appreciably alter the car's appraisal. In contrast, the presentation of the exemplar essay followed by the opposing editorial note giving statistical information significantly enhanced the quality evaluation of the car. Thus, first assessments based on statistical information were not altered by the subsequent presentation of exemplar information, whereas first assessments based on exemplar information were corrected by the presentation of statistical information. Base-rate information, then, being obtrusively presented as diametrically opposing the singular exemplification of an earlier received independent message, apparently exerted a greater degree of influence on judgments concerning the reliability and desirability of cars.

It should be clear that the findings of this investigation are limited to the sequential presentation of messages with opposing contents, and that they do not necessarily extend and apply to informational competition within particular messages. In this investigation, base-rate and exemplar information did not clash within the same message. Such possible integration of utterly contradictory claims would have little, if any, ecological validity; and it is, in fact, not to be found in journalistic practice or persuasive tactics (see chapter 2).

Krupat and associates (1997) replicated and extended their findings concerning the juxtaposition of claims and counterclaims made in successive messages by involving the evaluation of known foreign cars (Honda, Yugo). The reported effect emerged irrespective of familiarity with a particular make of car.

Krupat and associates (1997) interpreted their results as indicating "that base rate information will be used when it is comprehensible and *diagnostically relevant*" (p. 345, italics added). Earlier research had focused on the perceptual qualities (vividness, in particular) of base-rate presentations. The emphasis here is more on their diagnostic value for rendering judgment. The impression is given, however, that such value is inherent in base rates, and that it may apply only to "technical" cases in need of diagnostic scrutiny. It would appear that diagnostic scrutiny also can be driven by personal interest and especially by the salience that respondents attach to issues. For instance, a person with acute weight problems is more likely to pay close attention to, and to process base-rate information more carefully, than a person with a benevolent metabolism. Similarly, a person "addicted" to playing the stock market may absorb detailed statistics that will not reach most others. In all, it would seem outright foolish to claim that base rates are always dominated by exemplars. Surely there exist numerous conditions, many of which are yet to be specified, in which base rates will exert a dominant influence. This, however, does not detract from the fact that, concerning the news, most issues are at best moderately salient to recipients and consequently do not inspire much diagnostic scrutiny. Under these conditions, and also in view of the fact that in an information-rich environment laden with quantitative information not all specifics can be retained, the dominant influence of exemplification will be the rule rather than the exception.

In summary, given that little is known about the processing of base-rate information relative to that of exemplars as a function of salience, generalizations are limited to stimulus properties of base rates.

1. The influence of base-rate information can dominate that of exemplification.

2. Base-rate dominance is likely when the quantitative information is clearly articulated, perceptually enhanced, and when competing exemplar information is comparatively uninformative.

3. Base-rate dominance is likely when quantitative information has greater diagnostic relevance than exemplar presentation.

## Citation as Exemplar Enhancement

Whereas the linguistic manipulation of the presentation of exemplars in news reports has largely failed to produce appreciable effects, the syntactic variation of interviewee's articulations has been shown to have reliable effects. Specifically, it has been shown that letting people speak for themselves by explicitly citing their utterances leaves stronger impressions than having their statements paraphrased by the reporter. Exemplification in the I-format, then, appears to be more consequential than exemplification in the he-or-she format.

Gibson and Zillmann (1993, 1998) examined the effects of direct versus indirect citation on issue perception in print-news reports. In the initial investigation, three versions of a story about accidents at amusement parks were created. The control condition presented all pertinent facts about the year's accidents but did not feature interviews with victims. The other two conditions featured several victim interviews, these interviews being presented either in direct quotes or in paraphrased form. Testimony in direct quotes was, for instance:

> Julia Mosehart was hospitalized for several days after the metal bar securing the ferris wheel car fell onto her arm, tearing the skin and crushing one of the bones in her forearm. Mosehart said she was not the only passenger having problems with the metal bar. "I noticed other people on the ride having trouble with the safety bar, and some of the kids even left it unfastened because it was too heavy for them to pull down," she said. Mosehart said it took all of her strength just to move the bar. "Once I got the thing loosened, it was so heavy it just fell and crushed my arm," she reported. "In my opinion, safety equipment that causes injury instead of preventing it is not the best kind of equipment to have. It's inexcusable."

The same testimony in paraphrased form was:

> Julia Mosehart was hospitalized for several days after the metal bar securing the ferris wheel car fell onto her arm, tearing the skin and crushing one of the bones in her forearm. Mosehart said she noticed other passengers having trouble with the safety bar and that several children on the ride left it unfastened because it was too heavy for them to pull down. She said she had to use all of her strength just to get the bar to move, and then it was so heavy it fell and crushed her arm. Mosehart said she thought it inexcusable that the ride's safety equipment not only failed to prevent injury, but that it actually caused her to be hurt.

Respondents eventually indicated their own perceptions of the safety of rides and of the safety of coaster rides in particular.

The findings are summarized in Fig. 4.4. As can be seen, paraphrased testimonials exerted only a negligible effect on issue perception (compared against the control condition). Directly quoted testimony, on the other hand, resulted in a strong decline of the perception of the safety of rides at amusement parks. Letting people relate their experiences in their own words thus proved to influence issue perception more strongly than having their experiences conveyed by another person, a reporter in this case.

Interestingly, the presentation of these report versions as radio news failed to yield the described results. This failure may be due to the atypical format of the print report as radio news (i.e., its extreme length for radio). Alternatively, the act of reading may be more active and engaging, and it ultimately may make respondents more cognizant of the first-hand conveyance of experiences. The effects thus may be limited to reading.

The follow-up investigation (Gibson & Zillmann, 1998) manipulated a news-magazine report on the economics of family farming—similar to that described in

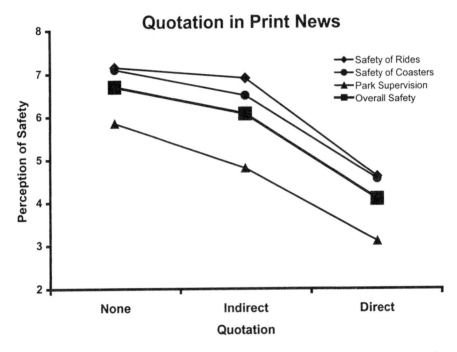

FIG. 4.4    Effects of direct versus indirect quotation (i.e., verbatim vs. paraphrased by reporting agent) of interviewees in a report on amusement-park safety. The interviews were with several victims of accidents incurred on rides. Direct quoting of their accounts of the accidents consistently produced perceptions of lesser safety than did the reporter's paraphrasing of the victims' statements. Authors' data, first published in "The impact of quotation in news reports on issue perception," by R. Gibson and D. Zillmann, 1993, *Journalism Quarterly, 70*(4), 793–800.

connection with the exemplar study by Zillmann and associates (1996). The report featured six interviews with farmers. Three were with poor farmers who lamented their demise, the other three were with rich farmers who hailed farming as greatly profitable. The report's text was identical in all conditions, except that some farmers' testimonies were quoted whereas others' were paraphrased. Specifically, in one condition, the interviews of both poor and rich farmers were presented in quotes; in another condition, both were presented in paraphrased form. More important, in one condition the poor farmers were quoted and the rich farmers were paraphrased. In a countercondition, the poor farmers were paraphrased and the rich farmers were quoted. As in the investigation detailed earlier, respondents estimated the relative incidence of family farms in financial difficulties and those that were prospering. In addition, the degree of the bankers' fault for the plight of poor farmers was ascertained.

   The findings, in part presented in Table 4.11, show that direct citation consistently fostered stronger effects than the same testimony in paraphrased form. In

TABLE 4.11
Effects of Direct Versus Indirect Quotation
of Exemplified Poor Farmers in Print News

|  | Quotation | |
| --- | --- | --- |
| Measure | Indirect | Direct |
| % of farmers losing money | 46.6[b] | 56.2[a] |
| % of farm bankruptcies | 23.4[b] | 33.1[a] |
| % of farmers making a profit | 44.1[a] | 34.8[b] |
| % of wealthy farmers | 21.9[a] | 13.8[b] |
| Banks at fault | 3.94[b] | 5.41[a] |
| Government at fault | 4.06[b] | 5.17[a] |

Note. Fault was assessed on a scale ranging from zero
to 10. Means having different superscripts differ significantly at $p < .05$. Comparisons are within measures only.
Authors' data, first published in "Effects of citation in
exemplifying testimony on issue perception," by R. Gibson and D. Zillmann, 1998, *Journalism & Mass Communication Quarterly, 75*(1), 167–176.

particular, citing poor farmers while paraphrasing rich farmers produced the
strongest indictments of banking practices as the cause for the poor farmers' misfortunes. In contrast, when citing rich farmers while paraphrasing poor farmers,
with their statements kept essentially identical, these practices received the least
criticism. Direct quotation, then, greatly enhanced the exemplars' effectiveness.
Citing appears to foster different processing and to increase the statements' salience. The information may be tagged as a reported primary experience, in contrast
to information recognized as a secondhand account. Such recognition might entail the perception of some degree of distortion by the reporter, which in turn
might diminish credence in comparison to unmitigated expression.

In summary, although the mediation of these citation effects remains unclear
and in need of elucidation, the following generalizations of the effects are possible:

1. Exemplars that feature personal testimony exert a stronger influence on issue perception when the testimony is expressed in direct quotes than when it is
paraphrased by the reporting agent.

2. At present, the citation effect specified in (1) appears to be specific to a reception mode (i.e., reading) or medium (i.e., print). The degree of the citation
effect's generality across modalities or media remains to be demonstrated.

## Qualitatively Distorted Exemplification

The earlier discussed quantitative misrepresentation by exemplar–counterexemplar
aggregations is complemented by qualitatively distorted exemplification. Perhaps

most typical of all misrepresentations in news reporting is the selection of just a few exemplars from the deviant side of occurrences under consideration, usually in the interest of more engaging and "sensational" reporting. Extraordinary, unusual, and bizarre cases, atypical by definition, tend to find their way into reports and potentially foster misperceptions of the addressed issues.

Gibson and Zillmann (1994) have examined the consequences of the indicated qualitative misrepresentation in print news. These investigators created and manipulated a magazine report on the crime of carjacking. The report, presented as a *Newsweek* article, provided either precise or vague base-rate information about this rather new crime. A survey was cited, stating (a) that 75% of all carjackings do not involve physical injury to the victims, (b) that 21% of the victims suffer minor injuries such as bruises, (c) that 3.8% of the victims incur severe bodily injury such as broken bones and major lacerations, and (d) that only an exceedingly small number of victims, 0.2%, is getting killed in the course of the commission of the crime. In the vague base-rate condition, the victim percentages were converted to (a) "most," (b) "some," (c) "only a few," and (d) "almost nobody."

Base-rate information was supplemented by two exemplars taken from one of the four victim categories. For instance, one of the exemplars detailed a carjacking at a gas station. A women had paid her bill and was ready to leave. She entered her car, only to be pushed out again by the carjacker, who usurped her car and drove off. In the no-injury version the text stated, "Adams was lucky. The incident terrified her, but she walked away without so much as a scratch." In the minor-injury version, the report read, "Adams was lucky. The incident terrified her, but she walked away with only minor cuts and bruises from falling onto the pavement." The severe-injury version stated, "Adams was fortunate, considering what could have happened. She was terrified, and she suffered a broken arm from being shoved out of the moving car and hitting the sharp edge of the gas pump." Finally, the death version explicated that:

> Unfortunately, Adams did not make it completely out of the car. Her arm got caught in the seatbelt as Block drove away, and she was dragged, screaming for help, for several feet alongside the car. As Block turned out of the station, Adams's head struck the curb, and she was killed instantly.

The carjacking article was one of three read by the respondents. Following the procedure detailed in connection with the investigation by Zillmann and associates (1992), respondents' issue perception was ascertained either shortly after reading or after a 1-week delay. Specifically, the respondents indicated their perceptions of the severity of the carjacking problem for the nation as well as their perceptions of their own risk of becoming a victim of this crime. They then estimated the percentages of various injuries incurred by victims of carjackings.

Ratings of the severity of carjacking as a national problem yielded the expected results. Exemplification of two cases of death made this crime appear to be a significantly greater threat to the nation than exemplification of all lesser outcomes.

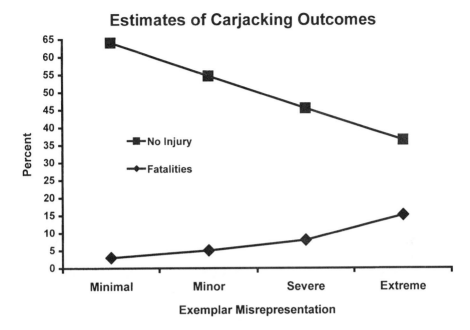

FIG. 4.5    Perception of carjackings that are injury-free or that result in the death of victims as a function of exemplification in a print-news article. The estimates are approximately correct (i.e., in accordance with provided base rates) in the condition of minimal injury in carjacking cases. Distortion in the perception of this crime increases with the degree of misrepresentation by the exemplars, with deadly outcomes being described in the extreme condition. Authors' data, first published in "Exaggerated versus representative exemplification in news reports: Perception of issues and personal consequences," by R. Gibson and D. Zillmann, 1993, *Communication Research, 21*(5), 603–624.

This effect was stable over time (i.e., over the 1-week delay period). On the other hand, base-rate information, whether vague or presented in precise terms, proved to be entirely inconsequential. Respondents once again based their perceptions of a vital social issue on exemplars rather than on more reliable base-rate information.

After reading about death from carjacking, respondents saw others at greater risk, but not themselves. Such invulnerability beliefs are readily explained, however, as the result of the students' living in an area in which carjackings are extremely unlikely.

Respondents' perceptions of the distributions of carjackings without injury and carjackings with deadly outcomes are summarized in Fig. 4.5. As can be seen, highly significant trends are as expected, showing a steady decline from minimal to extreme injury for injury-free carjackings and the reverse for carjackings with a deadly outcome. Base-rate information was again without consequence. In contrast, there was an unexpected effect of the delay of assessment. The exemplification effect increased, rather than diminishing over time.

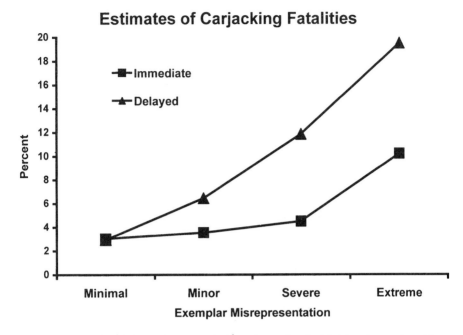

FIG. 4.6    The effect of exemplification on fatality estimates described in Fig. 4.5 over time. After 1 week, the misperception of carjacking outcomes caused by exemplar misrepresentation was stronger, not weaker, than immediately after exposure. Authors' data, first published in "Exaggerated versus representative exemplification in news reports: Perception of issues and personal consequences," by R. Gibson and D. Zillmann, 1993, *Communication Research, 21*(5), 603–624.

The pertinent findings are displayed in Fig. 4.6. As can be seen, the misperception created by the presentation of two rare and therefore atypical occurrences, namely carjackings with a deadly outcome, increased considerably with the passage of time. This *sleeper effect* is manifest in a significant trend from minimal to extreme distortion (the associated mean differences between immediate and delayed assessment were −0.09, 2.90, 7.36, and 9.29, respectively). Misperception thus increased with misrepresentation.

The explanation for this sleeper effect is straightforward. Exemplars of comparatively spectacular carjackings, those that entail broken bones and head smashing, are not forgotten and come more readily to mind than those of hapless carjackings. As the spectacular, threatening cases impose themselves from memory, with recall of associated abstract information fading over time, these cases increasingly dominate whatever corrective power base-rate information may initially have on the perception of issues. It should be remembered that the report of this investigation featured the most precise base-rate information in one of the base-rate conditions, and that this information was obtrusively presented at the outset. In creating perceptions, it was, nonetheless, readily overpowered by two exemplars that challenged and contradicted it. Most such issues are covered, however, without knowledge of the typicality or the atypicality of the exemplars selected for presentation. In these cases, the potential misrepresentation of the choice of spectacular exemplars goes entirely unchecked. Under these conditions, distorted issue perception can flourish and grow more extreme with the passage of time.

In summary, the following generalizations are possible.

1. Exemplification featuring atypical, spectacular, and sensational cases tends to foster distorted issue perceptions, even when supplemented with corrective base-rate information. Exemplification featuring rare and atypical occurrences invites the misperception of these occurrences as relatively frequent and typical, ultimately as normative.

2. The influence of exemplification that presents spectacular occurrences on issue perception can grow stronger over time, resulting in growing misperceptions.

### Emotional Displays in Exemplars

Broadcast news is partial to involving so-called reaction shots of people who express intense emotions. As the news favors threats, dangers, and disasters over fortuitous happenings (e.g., Haskins, 1984), shots of victims who express their despair and grief are likely to make the reports—in the name of "human interest." Footage of those who control their emotions in calm and collected interviews is not granted such human-interest value and is likely to end up in the editor's wastebasket. Exemplification thus is bound to convey a disproportional amount of human suffering in the form of adverse emotions displayed by victims and by their relatives and friends, as well as by witnesses to misfortunes and to catastrophes.

The consequences of emotion-laden exemplars for issue perception, the assessment of danger and risk in particular, have been examined by Aust and Zillmann (1996). Two broadcast-news reports were especially created and manipulated. One report concerned the risk of food poisoning; the other concerned the risk of becoming a victim of random violence. In both cases, a news anchor introduced the issue, and an on-location reporter provided a detailed account of an incident. For instance, in the story on food poisoning, the reporter was situated in front of a fast-food restaurant (of a national chain) in which customers had contracted salmonella poisoning. The reporter conveyed the essential facts about a retired couple who had died and about children, still hospitalized, in critical condition. In a control condition, this information constituted the entire report. In two additional conditions, interviews with the retirees' adult daughter and with the children's father, respectively, were incorporated in the report. These interviews were given either in nonemotional or in highly emotional fashion. In the interest of ecological validity, the text was derived from actual broadcasts. It was identical in both conditions. Emotionality was manipulated through the delivery of this text by experienced actors. Delivery was calm in the nonemotional conditions. The emotional delivery, in contrast, contained choked speech, pausing, heavy breathing, and fighting off tears, along with appropriate gestures and hand movements on the part of the men, and near-hysterical expressions, including overt crying, on the part of the women. The three report versions of the random-violence story were created analogously. The reporter was standing in front of another fast-food restaurant in which several persons had been shot arbitrarily by a disgruntled patron. The footage showed victims being rushed off on stretchers. The interviews again featured testimony in calm or in highly distressed fashion; for instance, that of a woman whose fiancé had been killed in the shooting.

The news stories were presented along with others on mail theft, on the discovery of dinosaur-skin fossils, and on the conservation of public lands. Respondents eventually indicated their perceptions of the severity of salmonella food poisoning and random handgun violence as national problems. They also assessed their own risk in response to the question, "How likely is it that you personally might become a victim of food poisoning/handgun violence?"

The findings are summarized in Fig. 4.7. As can be seen, the display of intense aversive emotions (under Upset) in news reports elevated both the perception of salmonella poisoning and of random violence as national problems and the assessment of associated risks to self above those of the control condition. These effects were significant. The incorporation of nonemotional testimony (under Calm), in contrast, although appearing to increase assessments of problem severity and risk, failed to be reliable.

Despite the provision of identical textual information, then, the nonverbally expressed emotionality in exemplars was found to exert considerable influence on risk perception in general as well as in specific, personal terms. It was observed that this influence is especially strong for highly empathic persons. Empathic sensitivity had been ascertained as a personality trait (Davis, 1983), and a median-split analysis revealed significant differences in affective reactions to the news revelations (Aust & Zillmann, 1996). Additionally, women, as they are generally more empathic than men, reacted especially strongly to these revelations. Moreover, gender differences were observed in risk assessment, with women's ratings indicating higher risk to others and to self than men's ratings.

An investigation by Hill and Zillmann (1999) extended these findings by showing that highly emotional testimony is also capable of influencing the moral assessment of social realities. The effects of talk shows typical of revealing circumstances that seem to mitigate any committed transgressions on the evaluation of these transgressions were examined. Specifically, programs were sampled from the *Oprah Winfrey Show,* as Oprah Winfrey is famed for her sympathetic and understanding treatment of delinquents whose offenses are thought to be traceable to predisposing abuses suffered earlier in their lives. Dershowitz (1994) contended that consumers of such programming fail to recognize the "junk science" status of the explanatory attempts, accept the "abuse excuse" in general terms, and become

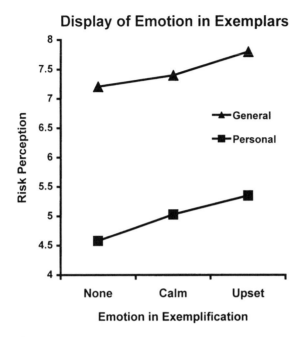

FIG. 4.7   The effect of unemotional (Calm) and emotional (Upset) exemplification of victimization by salmonella food poisoning and random handgun violence (combined). Emotional testimony by relatives and by friends of victims increased assessments of the danger to the nation (General) and the likelihood of personal victimization (Personal). Authors' data, first published in "Effects of victim exemplification in television news on viewer perception of social issues," by C. F. Aust and D. Zillmann, 1996, *Journalism & Mass Communication Quarterly, 73*(4), 787–803.

exceedingly lenient toward delinquents (p. 5). Focusing on the apparently growing leniency of Americans in the jury box, he argued that they "are beginning to behave like social workers" (cited in Leo, 1994, p. 17).

Hill and Zillmann (1999) tested the merits of these suggestions by manipulating two *Oprah* programs, one about a mother who executed the presumed sexual molester of her 6-year-old son as it became clear that a conviction was not forthcoming and the other about a father who refused to pay child support for his two children because of numerous difficulties with his estranged former wife. The cases, though vastly different regarding the criminal transgressions involved, were parallel in that both programs featured ample mitigating exemplars that made the court-prescribed punishment seem unwarranted and even unjust. For instance, the mother had been found guilty of voluntary manslaughter and was serving a 10-year term in a women's facility. The program featured interviews with the mother and her two children, a son and a daughter. The testimony of all was highly emotional, especially that of the children. The boy, the alleged victim, recounted the abusive experiences and his being suicidal. He described the victimization of four other boys and revealed death threats to prevent disclosure of the abuse. He expressed satisfaction about the molester's death and stated that he now feels safe. A repeated argument was that the molester would no longer be able to sodomize other children. The daughter underscored this justification of the molester's death and, by implication, of his being killed by her mother. Much love was expressed between mother, son, and daughter. The children claimed to need their mother desperately and suggested that her continued incarceration would serve no purpose. Tears were shed most of the time during the interviews. Oprah probed why the mother had "snapped" and killed after such severe provocation, and she radiated sympathy with the children and their desire to be reunited with their mother. The testimony in the child-support case was less gut-wrenching, but it also entailed emotional pleas.

Both programs were manipulated by removing the transgression-mitigating information in the emotional testimony. The versions without mitigating information simply presented Oprah's introduction of the issue; that is, of the circumstances of the crime and its punishment. Her introduction may have indicated some degree of sympathy for the delinquents as "victims" of apparently unjust legal rulings. A no-exposure control condition was employed in addition to exposure to the two programs with and without emotional exemplification.

In the no-exposure condition and following exposure in the two manipulated program conditions (after the two programs within these conditions had been evaluated for informativeness to provide closure on the talk-show study), a second investigator, purportedly conducting unrelated legal research for the American Bar Association, was introduced to the respondents. This investigator presented six vignettes of nonviolent and violent crimes, covering burglary, rape, embezzlement, murder, arson, and attempted murder. Respondents were asked to recommend a prison term for each crime, a term they thought appropriate under the specified circumstances. The administrator of the media part of the investigation returned eventually and had the respondents who had seen the manipulated *Oprah* programs indicate their reactions to the presented cases.

Not surprisingly, both the manslaughter and the child-support case fostered greater leniency when presented with emotionally displayed mitigating information than when this information was removed. Incarceration recommendations were significantly lower (by about 2 years in either case) when mitigating information was present than when it was not. Judgments of the delinquents' irresponsibility and the sentences' unfairness varied accordingly.

The focus of this investigation was not, however, on Oprah's success in fostering lenient dispositions toward the delinquents featured in her programs. It was, instead, on whether such a lenient "mind set" extends beyond these cases. The pivotal question was the following: Does the emotional exemplification of delinquents who provide much justification for "reaching the breaking point" and,

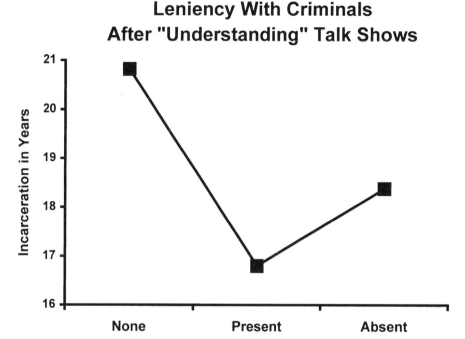

## Leniency With Criminals
## After "Understanding" Talk Shows

FIG. 4.8    The effect of emotion-laden testimony on moral assessments of criminal conduct. Incarceration recommendations for various nonviolent and violent crimes were made after exposure to episodes of the *Oprah Winfrey Show* in which the criminal-justice system was portrayed as excessively punitive toward delinquents whose transgressive actions were analyzed and "understood" in terms of predisposing abuses. Respondents were either not preexposed to the programs in a control condition (None) or saw two manipulated programs that either featured emotionally displayed mitigating information (Present) or were devoid of such information (Absent). Authors' data, first published in "The Oprahization of America: Sympathetic crime talk and leniency, " by J. R. Hill and D. Zillmann, 1999, *Journal of Broadcasting & Electronic Media, 43*(1), 67–82.

hence, for losing control over their actions, and who express the conviction that their punishment is unjust and ineffective, if not counterproductive, along with the apparent approval and endorsement by sympathetic show hosts, create lenient dispositions toward crime at large?

The findings, summarized in Fig. 4.8, are supportive of this conjecture. As can be seen, incarceration recommendations for all six crimes considered were markedly lower after exposure to *Oprah* programs that portrayed delinquents as victims of an overly punitive, if not inhumane, criminal-justice system than after no exposure to such programs. This effect was observed for both nonviolent and violent crimes, irrespective of the fact that the sentences for violent crimes were significantly higher than those for nonviolent ones. The effect of the mitigation-absent condition, though not significant, suggests that Oprah's introduction of the cases may have projected miscarriages of justice and a distrust of the criminal-justice system and that this information alone may have exerted some degree of influence on the evaluation of other crimes.

The findings reported by Hill and Zillmann (1999) thus establish that considerations of justice, essentially the moral assessment of conduct under specific motivational circumstances, can be influenced by exemplification that involves emotional displays. The creation of dispositions of leniency toward perpetrators of crimes, in particular, has been shown to generalize from media exemplification to extramedia realities.

In summary, the findings, taken together, show that assessments of the severity of dangers to the public and of associated personal risks, when made during empathic distress or in its aftermath, yield higher estimates than when such assessments are made in nonemotional states. The fact that empathic sensitivity enhances both the affective reaction to news revelations and the subsequent risk assessment further implicates emotionality in the effect on risk perception. The following generalizations thus may be offered.

1. News reports that engage the respondents' empathy with the display of aversive emotions by victims and their affiliates are likely to foster higher estimates of risks to others and to self than reports without such displays.

2. Empathic sensitivity enhances the effect specified in (1).

3. The effect specified in (1) is stronger for women than for men, mostly because of women's greater empathic sensitivity.

4. Emotion-laden exemplification is capable of influencing moral assessments of conduct. The portrayal of emotional upheaval and grief of victims, in particular, is likely to foster sympathy that, in cases where the victims committed transgressions, motivates leniency toward such victims.

## Threatening Images in Exemplification

Threatening images in the news have long been thought capable of stirring emotions and foster public outcry like few, if any, alternative means of expression (cf. Sharkey, 1993). For instance, images of the impromptu execution of a Viet Cong prisoner in the streets of Saigon by Brig. Gen. Nguyen Ngoc Loan are believed to have severely shocked the American citizenry and fueled antiwar sentiment across the nation. More recently, news images, in the form of both photographs and film footage, appear to have dictated U.S. foreign policy concerning Somalia (Zillmann, 1997). A barrage of images of starved, grotesquely deformed, near-death Somali children and adults prompted Americans to pressure their government to intervene in Somalia. This pressure is thought to have produced the intended action. As the intervention failed to squelch the famine and internal power rivalries, however, and especially as the public was confronted with images of jeering Somalis dragging the body of a dead U.S. soldier through the streets of Mogadishu, kicking it and spitting on it, the sentiment reversed. Public pressure now called for immediate withdrawal from Somalia, and it also yielded the intended action. Instances of similarly powerful image effects abound, all sharing the premise that they could not have been created by even the most articulate verbal account of the pictured events (cf. Gerbner, 1992; Johnson-Cartee & Copeland, 1991; Messaris, 1997).

Despite the plausibility that the causal attribution of effects to ubiquitous displays of "compelling," threatening images may have in historical contexts, acceptable proof of such image effects has been wanting. Moreover, it has remained rather unclear what it is that makes a threatening image compelling. Compellingness is usually granted in retrospect (i.e., after an image is thought to have generated a dramatic effect). The concept thus tends to be circularly applied.

Regarding the acquisition and retention of text and image integrating information involved in the mediation of issue perception, investigations by Graber (1990), Brosius (1993), Wanta and Roark (1993), and Brosius, Donsbach, and Birk (1996) leave no doubt about the fact that text-consistent images enhance text-defined news recall. Redundancy in the display of relevant occurrences is particularly effective in facilitating the recall of these occurrences. However, the involvement of emotion-evoking images is effective only to the extent that the images portray pivotal events. The involvement of extrafocal emotional imagery has been shown to be counterproductive because it draws disproportional attention to itself, this at the expense of attention to the focal information (cf. Brosius, 1993; Mundorf, Drew, Zillmann, & Weaver, 1990).

The effects of threatening images in broadcast news on issue perception were investigated by Zillmann and Gan (1996). These investigators manipulated a CNN health broadcast designed to appraise sunbathers of the danger of contracting skin cancer. The broadcast was aired prior to the onset of summer vacation and targeted adolescents headed for the beaches. It started with beach scenes of sunbathers and soon turned to the risks associated with extended sun exposure. The etiology of melanoma was explained by several dermatologists. The risks accruing to excessive sunbathing were detailed; and the benefits of protective measures, such as the use of sunblock lotions, were discussed. Victim testimony was interspersed. In the original broadcast, the sunburned shoulder of one victim was shown, along with a minor case of melanoma (dime-sized) on the arm. Although death from melanoma was discussed in connection with another case, the described imagery seemed sanitized and nonthreatening. It provided the opportunity for image manipulation without altering the text in any way. A condition of threatening imagery thus was created by replacing the described nonthreatening scene with footage depicting a victim's shoulder largely covered by melanoma skin cancer and indication of the surgical removal of basal and squamous cell carcinoma. The newscast ended with a caution and the recommendation to use sunblock lotions when sunbathing.

Respondents were exposed to a series of four news reports dealing with handgun violence, World Cup Soccer, melanoma from excessive sun exposure (one of the two versions), and a train derailment. After each report, they evaluated the newsworthiness of the newscast. Along with these evaluations, they indicated their emotional reactions to the report.

In a condition of immediate effect assessment, the respondents then were introduced to another investigator who conducted, purportedly so, a General Health Survey that included queries about the risk of specific injury from various athletic and recreational activities. Respondents also indicated the usefulness of particular precautions in preventing injury. Embedded in this survey were questions concerning the melanoma risk from excessive sun exposure to the public and to self. Attached to the risk assessment was the evaluation of the need for protection against melanoma by use of sunblock lotions. In the condition of delayed effect assessment, the administration of this survey was delayed by 2 weeks.

The results revealed, first of all, that the incorporation of threatening images created a threatening report. On a zero (not at all) to 10 (extremely) point scale, the report featuring the threatening images averaged 8.80. The same report containing the sanitized images averaged 7.69, showing that this version was by no means nonthreatening. Nonetheless, inclusion of the stark images significantly increased the threat conveyed by the melanoma report.

The immediate and delayed effects of the two health programs on the perception of melanoma as a threat to public health are displayed in Fig. 4.9. As can be seen, the immediate impact actually favored the sanitized program version, but not significantly so. The suggestion of an immediately weaker effect of the threatening images might be explained by their novelty. Respondents may have been surprised by the explicit nature of the "medical footage" and, expecting to see sanitized imagery, thought that the threatening images were overly distressing and unnecessary. However, the threatening images exerted themselves most compellingly in the delayed assessment. Two weeks after exposure to the programs, the version featuring threatening images yielded risk estimates that markedly exceeded those of the version with sanitized images. The observed absolute sleeper effect is consistent with the proposal that threatening images, in particular, continue to impose themselves in memory, whereas the accessibility of alternative information, especially of comparatively abstract forms, diminishes over time. These findings add to the evidence of sleeper effects in issue perception discussed in connection with the investigation by Gibson and Zillmann (1994; see also this volume, chapter 4, the section titled "Qualitatively Distorted Exemplification").

Figure 4.10 summarizes the findings concerning the assessment of personal risk and the perceived need for protection. As can be seen, both personal risk and protection need are at similar levels immediately after exposure. The report, even

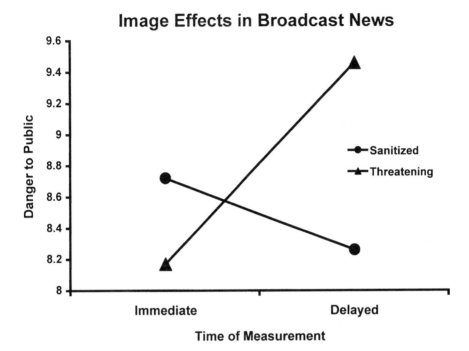

FIG. 4.9    Perception of danger to the beach-going public from excessive sunbathing as a function of exposure to a health broadcast featuring sanitized or threatening images of skin cancer and of time of assessment after exposure to the broadcast (short vs. 2-week delay). The sleeper effect of exposure to the threatening newscast is evident in the diverging gradients. After exposure to the news that featured threatening images, estimates of danger increased over time; after exposure to the sanitized version, it did not. The apparent effect decline after exposure to the sanitized version proved to be negligible. Authors' data, first published in "Effects of threatening images in news programs on the perception of risk to others and self," by D. Zillmann and S. Gan, 1996, *Medienpsychologie: Zeitschrift für Individual- und Massenkommunikation, 8*(4), 288–305, 317–318.

when featuring sanitized images, apparently was informative and scary enough to make beach-loving students realize that they themselves are at appreciable risk of contracting melanoma from excessive sun exposure. Along with that realization, they accepted the need to protect themselves with sunblock lotion when sunbathing. The sleeper effect of delayed exposure differs, however, from that concerning the assessment of danger to the public. The downward-directed divergent interaction defines a *relative sleeper effect.* Instead of a growing effect of public-risk perception after exposure to threatening images, the effect of exposure to sanitized images diminished with time. That is to say that the newscast featuring threatening images retained its effect over time, presumably because the imagery imposed itself at later times and continued to reinstate the severe consequences of excessive sun exposure. The newscast featuring sanitized images, in contrast, lost its

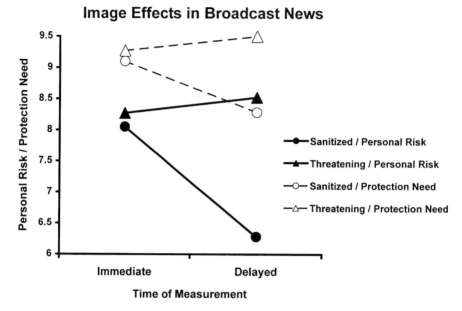

FIG. 4.10    Personal risk of contracting, and need for protection against, skin cancer from excessive sun exposure. Over time, the effects of the threatening broadcast proved to be stable, whereas those of the sanitized broadcast deteriorated markedly. Authors' data, first published in "Effects of threatening images in news programs on the perception of risk to others and self," by D. Zillmann and S. Gan, 1996, *Medienpsychologie: Zeitschrift für Individual- und Massenkommunikation, 8*(4), 288–305, 317–318.

influence on issue perception—presumably because accessibility of these images deteriorated along with that of the other health information.

The influence of threatening images is, of course, not limited to the depiction of consequences of disease, of violent conflict, or of natural disasters. The expression of deep hatred and the associated intent to harm would seem to produce similar effects. Gan and colleagues (1996) demonstrated as much in an investigation of the television-news coverage of the 1994 Hebron massacre in which an Israeli settler gunned down Islamic worshippers in a mosque. Some news reports, after presenting scenes of the aftermath of the shooting, featured interviews with Israeli extremists who praised the killing as "a good beginning" and "a courageous, moral act." Other reports highlighted Israeli Prime Minister Yitzak Rabin who condemned the massacre in no uncertain terms and confessed that "as a Jew and an Israeli, as a man and a human being, I am humiliated by the shame brought upon us by the lowly killer" (Knesset resolution, 1994). The available news footage was immediately re-edited to create news reports about the massacre as such (i.e., without exemplification), a version featuring action-endorsing interviews in addition, a version featuring the condemnation of the action instead, and a version including both endorsing and condemning positions.

Following exposure to one of these reports, respondents indicated their perceptions of the prospect of peace in the Middle East. They estimated, among other things, the population proportion of Israelis pursuing the violent suppression of Palestinians versus the proportion committed to compromise in the interest of lasting peace.

The results are shown in Fig. 4.11. As can be seen, the presentation of five interviews with Israeli extremists convinced respondents that a majority of Israelis prefer war over peace. Interviews expressive of deep hatred, such as the characterization of the massacre as "a loyal act of heroism on behalf of the Jewish people" by the founder of the Kahane Chai organization, apparently leave profound impressions that exert disproportional influence on judgment. Apologies, no matter how

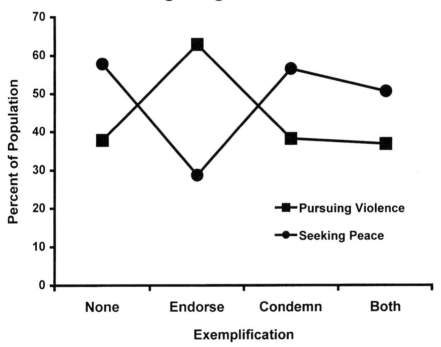

FIG. 4.11    Estimates of Israelis seeking peace with the Palestinians versus those pursuing oppression by violent means as a function of newscasts featuring interviews with Israeli extremists celebrating the Hebron massacre of Palestinian worshippers in a mosque (Endorse), with Israelis deploring the massacre as a heinous crime against humanity (Condemn), or with exemplars of both sides (Both). Authors' data, first published in "The Hebron massacre, selective reports of Jewish reactions, and perceptions of volatility in Israel," by S. Gan, J. R. Hill, E. Pschernig, and D. Zillmann, 1996, *Journal of Broadcasting and Electronic Media, 40,* 122–131.

sincere, do not seem to convey such deep emotion. It should also be noted that a balanced presentation of spiteful dispositions and expressions of regret is likely to prevent the distorting effect on perception and judgment that the sheer dwelling on emotionally extreme, atypical, and sensational exemplars tends to have.

The effects on issue perception of threatening images in print-news articles have been examined by Zillmann, Gibson, and Sargent (1999). The article on the safety of amusement parks, on the risk of riding coasters in particular (as used by Gibson & Zillmann, 1993; see the section of this chapter titled "Citation as Exemplar Enhancement"), was presented either without photographs in a control condition, with a threatening photograph showing an accident victim on a stretcher being placed into an ambulance in front of a coaster, with a nonthreatening photograph showing ecstatic children on a coaster ride, or with both of these photographs. The text, featuring interviews with accident victims but also providing information to the effect that rides are safer than ever before, was identical in all conditions. Respondents indicated their perceptions of park safety and their personal safety concerns either shortly after reading or after a 10-day delay.

The findings, shown in Fig. 4.12, show that the threatening image markedly altered the perception of general safety and personal concerns. Specifically, the presence of this image fostered assessments of lesser safety and greater personal concerns. Moreover, this image effect was stable over the 10-day delay period. It had been expected that the photograph of ecstatic children would diminish concerns about the safety of rides. This image was without appreciable effect, however, presumably because it signaled carefree joy rather than coaster safety.

In an investigation by Gibson and Zillmann (1999; see also Zillmann, 1998, and the section of this chapter titled "Incidental Pictorial Exemplification"), a print-news report on a fictitious new tick disease moving down the Appalachian Mountains into North Carolina and into adjacent states was presented with or without menacing-looking ticks. Specifically, a New England and an Appalachian tick, with minor differences between them, were depicted in one version of the *Health & Medicine* story titled "Ticks cutting a mean path: Areas in the Southeast hardest hit by deadly new disease." The report indicated that children were the principal victims of the fictitious disease.

Respondents eventually estimated the risk of contracting the new disease for children of various ethnic groups in the tick-infested regions. These estimates were consistently higher after exposure to the version featuring the image of the two ticks. The overall difference was highly significant ($M = 4.2$ for the story without the image; $M = 5.6$ for that with the image, the ratings being on a zero (not at all at risk) to 10 (very much at risk) point scale).

The image of the ticks not only increased risk estimates, but it apparently fostered more careful reading of the text in addition. In an information acquisition test on the symptoms of the new disease, respondents who had been exposed to the story version with the image of the ticks performed significantly better than those who had read the same text without the image. On a 20-item test, the image group

# Image Effects in Print News

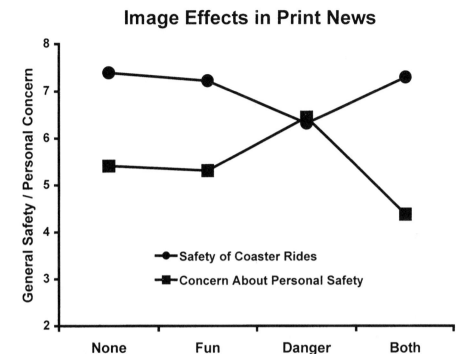

FIG. 4.12    The effect of threatening images, short and long term, in print news on issue perception. The critical, threatening image (Danger) depicted an injured person on a stretcher being moved into an ambulance in front of a roller coaster. The nonthreatening image (Fun) showed ecstatic children riding a roller coaster. Authors' data, first published in "Effects of photographs in news-magazine reports on issue perception," by D. Zillmann, R. Gibson, and S. L. Sargent, 1999, *Media Psychology, 3,* 207–228.

averaged 11.09 correct responses; the text-only group averaged only 8.28 correct responses. This finding suggests that threatening images not only impose themselves when related judgments are rendered but signal salience that in turn instigates curiosity and vigilance that ultimately yields superior acquisition of relevant information.

In summary, images conveying threats and dangers appear to constitute a domain of imagery capable of exerting especially strong influence on judgment and on the assessment of risk in particular. The following generalizations can be offered.

1. Threatening images, compared to nonthreatening ones, increase the perception of image-related risk to the public. The effect tends to persist over time. On occasion, the effect grows with the passage of time, thereby creating an absolute sleeper effect.

2. Threatening images, compared to nonthreatening ones, increase the assessment of image-related personal risk. This effect also tends to persist over time. The effect of nonthreatening images is less stable and deteriorates with the passage of time, thereby creating a relative sleeper effect.

3. The unopposed use of threatening images can lead to gross misassessments of threatening conditions.

4. Threatening images appear to arouse curiosity and vigilance, thereby facilitating the acquisition of information about threatening conditions.

### Effects of Innocuous Images

Innocuous images may not have the power of threatening images in stirring emotions, thereby influencing the perception of phenomena, but they should, nonetheless, draw initial attention to themselves and then influence the information acquisition from texts. A photograph of ecstatic coaster riders, for instance, may be irrelevant as far as the safety–danger dimension is concerned but may appreciably bias the perception of amusements to be had at parks toward "great fun." Especially with the passage of time, such a photograph may assume dominant influence over text revelations of mishaps.

Research by Grimes (1990) provides evidence that the information presented in image–text admixtures tends to combine and fuse as suggested. In a paradigm-setting study, Pezdek (1977) demonstrated that the information of simultaneously presented verbal statements (e.g., "The bird was perched atop the tree.") and images (e.g., of an eagle perched atop a tree) merged over time (i.e., respondents believed the sentence to have been "An eagle was perched atop the tree."). Grimes applied this research paradigm to a television-news report in which statements coincided with particular images. In a report on dating services, the text stated, for instance, that daters do not reveal many of their vices. The simultaneously presented imagery showed a student with a gin bottle in his back pocket. After a 2-day delay, respondents recalled the text as essentially stating that daters do not reveal their alcoholism, among other vices.

These and related findings (e.g., Grimes & Drechsel, 1996) show that the footage underlying texts in broadcast news is by no means inconsequential for issue perception, and they urge against the careless combination of image and text in the interest of "livelier" reports.

Zillmann and associates (1999) investigated the indicated merging of information from text–image admixtures, especially the expected merger over time, in print news. The story on the economics of family farming (see the sections titled "Exemplar–Counterexemplar Distributions" and "Citation as Exemplar Enhancement" of this chapter) was slightly altered to accomplish an exemplar balance between poor and rich farmers. The report was titled "New American Farmers Telling Tales of Poverty and Riches." With the text kept identical, four image versions were created: a control condition without photographs, a version with a photograph of a poor farmer, one with a photograph of a wealthy farmer, and one with both of these photographs. The images were entirely nonthreatening. The poor-farmer photograph showed a slender farmer walking behind a horse-drawn dated farming implement. The rich-farmer photograph presented a well-nourished farmer posturing in front of his new supertruck and private airplane.

Respondents read the article along with other reports. Shortly after reading or after a 10-day delay they indicated their perceptions of farming economics. Specifically, they estimated the percentages of poor farmers losing money and going into bankruptcy and the percentage of rich farmers making good money and getting wealthy.

The findings are summarized in Table 4.12. As can be seen, the images failed to exert appreciable influence shortly after reading. The balanced text was apparently well recalled at this time, a circumstance that prevented distorting image effects. After 10 days, however, the images exerted their expected influence and shifted perception in the direction of their content. The poor-farmer image fostered an overestimation of money-losing farmers headed for bankruptcy. In contrast, the rich-farmer image led to an overestimation of the prevalence of wealthy farmers. Additionally, the poor-farmer depiction fostered an absolute sleeper effect. It should be noticed, moreover, that the balanced photographic exemplification did not lead to distorted perceptions. Means of the condition presenting both photographs were not appreciably different from those of the no-image control condition.

TABLE 4.12

Estimated Incidence of Poor and Rich Farmers as a Function
of Photographic Images in a Report on the Economics of Farming

| Measures | Farmer Portrayal by Image | | | |
|---|---|---|---|---|
| | None | Poor | Rich | Poor + Rich |
| % poor farmers | | | | |
| Immediate | 34.2 | $36.0^x$ | $36.8^y$ | 37.2 |
| Delayed | $34.2^a$ | $44.2^{b,y}$ | $28.7^{a,x}$ | $31.8^a$ |
| % rich farmers | | | | |
| Immediate | 30.3 | 31.5 | 34.7 | 27.2 |
| Delayed | $28.2^a$ | $25.6^a$ | $37.6^b$ | $32.6^a$ |

*Note.* The poor farmer percentage combines estimates of farms losing money and farmers going into bankruptcy. The rich farmer percentage combines estimates of profitable farms and farmers getting wealthy. Comparisons between means denoted by *a–b* superscripts are across image conditions (horizontal). Comparisons between means denoted by *x–y* superscripts are across time (vertical). Means with different superscripts differ significantly at $p < .05$. There were no significant differences in the immediate effects. Authors' data, first published in "Effects of photographs in news-magazine reports on issue perception," by D. Zillmann, R. Gibson, and S. L. Sargent, 1999, *Media Psychology, 3,* 207–228.

The effect of aggregating different numbers of innocuous images in connection with exemplification text about potentially threatening issues has been examined by Perkins (1999). This investigator created broadcast-news reports on mothers' protest of the distribution of horror videos (based on R. L. Stein's highly successful *Goosebumps* books for children) by public libraries, and on home owners' concerns about radon gas in their homes. In both cases, an anchor introduced the issue, and several persons expressed their stand on it. This was followed by an opposing position taken by an official source and a closing statement by the anchor. The *Goosebumps* story presented eight arguments favoring the removal of the videos from the library shelves. The arguments pointed to ill effects on the children, such as restlessness, hyperactivity, and rough play, but also sleeplessness because of nightmares. The radon story also presented eight arguments, all focusing on health problems and financial difficulties caused by the presence of the gas. These arguments were kept constant in all experimental conditions. The only variation concerned the number of persons uttering them. This number varied from two to four to eight. That is, the exemplar portion of the *Goosebumps* news report presented either two, four, or eight mothers who pleaded their case for the removal of the videos. Likewise, the radon story featured either two, four, or eight home owners expressing their concerns. The somewhat threatening text was identical overall. It was articulated, however, by different numbers of visually innocuous speakers. All speakers, moreover, had been pretested to ensure that they were similarly appealing, intelligent, and credible.

It was expected that the effect of the overall identical information would increase with the number of persons delivering it. For instance, seeing eight mothers plead their case should leave the impression that many mothers are concerned about the videos in question, perhaps even that the issue is of great social importance—as many are moved to unpopular action. The delivery of the same arguments by only two mothers, in contrast, might leave the impression that a few mothers see fault with the videos, and that the issue is one of a few overly concerned moms. The same reasoning applies to deriving expectations for the effects of the radon gas story.

Table 4.13 displays the effects of the *Goosebumps* report. As can be seen, all relevant effects were as expected. The argument presentation by eight mothers led to perceptions of greater likelihood and incidence of ill effects on children, as well as stronger support for the removal of the videos from libraries, than did the presentation by two mothers. Delivery by four mothers produced intermediate results. It should be noted that respondents were mostly mothers with children of the age of *Goosebumps* video consumers.

As can be seen from Table 4.14, the radon gas report fostered essentially the same differentiation between two and eight presenters. The four-presenter condition, however, was not intermediate. For magnitude estimates (i.e., how dangerous/important . . . ?), the four-source and the eight-source conditions had comparable effects; in contrast, for incidence estimation, effects of the two-source and

## TABLE 4.13
Mothers' Estimates of Ill Effects of Horror Videos on Children
and Opposition to Public Library Distribution of the Videos
as a Function of Television News Featuring Different Numbers
of Pleading Mothers Providing Identical Information

| | Complementary Exemplars | | |
| Measure | Two | Four | Eight |
|---|---|---|---|
| Ill effects on all children | 4.25[a] | 5.08[ab] | 6.10[b] |
| Ill effects on own children | 4.08[a] | 5.28[ab] | 6.04[b] |
| Support of video removal | 3.41[a] | 4.52[a] | 5.33[b] |
| % children affected | 24.6[a] | 27.6[a] | 39.5[b] |

*Note.* Except for percentage estimates, ratings are on 0 to 10
point scales. The ratings concern perceptions of the likelihood of
adverse effects of the videos, such as hyperactivity and rowdiness,
as well as opposition to the videos' presence in public libraries.
Comparisons are within measures only. Means not sharing a superscripts differ significantly at $p < .05$. All linear trends of this differentiation are also significant at that level. From *Effects of information source quantity and personal experience in issue exemplification*,
1999, by J. W. Perkins, Jr., unpublished doctoral dissertation,
University of Alabama, Tuscaloosa. Adapted with permission.

## TABLE 4.14
Home Owners' Estimates of the Danger of Radon Gas in Homes, the Importance
of Testing their Residence for the Gas, and Loss of Property Value in Case
of its Presence as a Function of Television News Featuring Different Numbers
of Concerned Home Owners Providing Identical Information

| | Complementary Exemplars | | |
| Measure | Two | Four | Eight |
|---|---|---|---|
| Danger of radon gas | 5.88[a] | 7.72[b] | 7.72[b] |
| Importance of residence test | 5.07[a] | 6.94[b] | 6.85[b] |
| % loss of property value | 11.9[a] | 17.5[a] | 46.2[b] |

*Note.* Except for percentage estimates, ratings are on 0 to 10
point scales. The ratings concern perceptions of the degree of danger posed by radon gas and the importance of protective testing.
Comparisons are within measures only. Means not sharing a superscripts differ significantly at $p < .05$. From *Effects of information
source quantity and personal experience in issue exemplification*,
1999, by J. W. Perkins, Jr., unpublished doctoral dissertation,
University of Alabama, Tuscaloosa. Adapted with permission.

the four-source conditions were comparable. It should be noted again that the respondents were mostly home owners.

Taken together, the effects of both broadcast-news reports give strong evidence that the sheer number of concrete, visible sources relating their experiences and concerns does exert an influence on issue perception. Specifically, estimates of both the incidence and the salience of relevant phenomena tend to increase with the number of exemplifying sources.

In summary, effects of innocuous images have been ascertained for print and for broadcast news. They may be summarized as follows.

1. The use of photographs with innocuous content in print news may have little effect on issue perception as long as recipients are cognizant of much of the information conveyed by the associated text. Over time, however, such cognizance diminishes, therefore allowing the retained image to influence the perception of issues. With the passage of time, then, issue perception is likely to shift in the direction of image content.

2. Issue perception is influenced by the number of visually innocuous sources of information in broadcast news. Specifically, relevant incidence estimates and estimates of issue salience tend to increase with the number of sources—independent of the information that these sources provide. The linearity of this relationship is unlikely to extend to markedly larger exemplar numbers (i.e., above eight). The point at which their effect levels off is presently not known, however.

### Incidental Pictorial Exemplification

The consequences of the incidental placement of image exemplars into remotely related text have been explored primarily in a legal context. Broadcast news is known to embellish text presentations with footage to "liven up" the story. This footage is often drawn from archives and, hence, is not specific to reported happenings. Such practice may be inconsequential in many cases. On occasion, however, it may foster unintended connections, especially defamatory ones, that prompt libel suits from parties rendered "guilty by association." Grimes and Drechsel (1996) described cases, such as a report on a newly filed medical-negligence suit that was juxtaposed with archival footage of a medical procedure properly performed by an arbitrarily picked gynecologist, in which the plaintiffs could convincingly demonstrate damage and be awarded compensation.

The often careless, incidental involvement of imagery may also have implications, however, for issue perception. This possibility has been examined in an investigation by Gibson and Zillmann (1999; see also Zillmann, 1998, and the section titled "Threatening Images in Exemplification" of this chapter). A news-magazine report about a fictitious Appalachian tick disease was created and supplemented with various threatening and innocuous images. The story projected the spreading of the disease through the Appalachian Mountains in North Carolina and in neighboring states. Children were said to be its primary victims. The text, identical in all experimental conditions, detailed symptoms of the disease and compared them to those of the Lyme disease of New England and the Rocky Mountains. What the text did not say is of particular importance: It made no reference to the child victims' ethnicity. It also veiled the children's gender.

A control condition of the report did not include images. A condition already described in the section titled "Threatening Images in Exemplification" featured an image of two ticks (i.e., the New England variety and the fictitious new one). Three additional conditions presented three child victims. The photographs showed similarly attractive children happy at play or in school, obviously prior to their contracting the disease. The entirely incidental variation concerned the children's ethnicity. The three children either were all White, all Black, or two White and one Black—in efforts at approximating the ethnicity proportion of the population.

Respondents who had read one of the various versions of the article eventually indicated their perception of the danger of the new disease. They also estimated the risk of contracting the disease by age group and by region. The focal measure was the risk estimation for ethnic groups. Whites and Blacks were, of course, of central interest. Risk estimates for Hispanic Americans and for Asian Americans were not expected to be influenced by the incidental image exemplification. These ethnic groups were included mainly to disguise the research interest. It should be recalled that the text gave no hint about the disease's distribution among ethnic subpopulations, such that any differences in the risk estimates for ethnic groups are attributable only to the incidentally placed images.

The findings on this focal measure are displayed in Table 4.15. As can be seen, the incidental image exemplification had marked effects. The threatening image of the two ticks, as already detailed in the previously mentioned section, significantly

TABLE 4.15

Perception of the Risk of Disease from Tick Bite for Different Ethnic Populations as a Function of Ethnically Specific Pictorial Victim Exemplification

| | Pictorial Exemplars | | | | |
|---|---|---|---|---|---|
| Population | None | Ticks | White + Black | White | Black |
| Whites | 5.06[a] | 6.35[b] | 7.62[bc] | 8.03[c] | 6.57[b] |
| Blacks | 4.44[a] | 5.96[b] | 7.58[c] | 6.37[b] | 7.97[c] |

Note. Victim exemplification includes the image of ticks. Comparisons between means are within population only (horizontal). Means not sharing a superscript letter differ significantly at $p < .05$. Authors' data, from Reading between the photographs: The influence of incidental pictorial information on issue perception, by R. Gibson and D. Zillmann, D., 1999 (August), paper presented to the Visual Communication Division of the Association for Education in Journalism and Mass Communication at the national conference, New Orleans, LA.

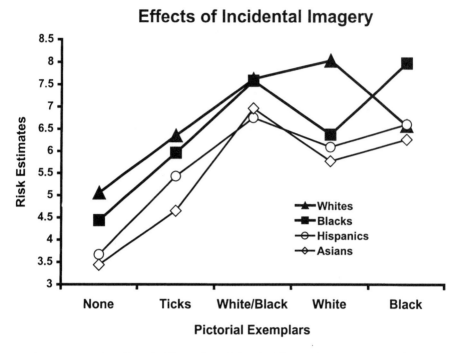

FIG. 4.13    Perception of the risk of disease from tick bite for different ethnic populations as a function of ethnically specific pictorial victim exemplification. Three victim exemplars are featured in addition to the image of ticks. Authors' data, from *Reading between the photographs: The influence of incidental pictorial information on issue perception,* by R. Gibson and D. Zillmann, D., 1999 (August), paper presented to the Visual Communication Division of the Association for Education in Journalism and Mass Communication at the national conference, New Orleans, LA.

elevated risk assessments. It did so irrespective of the ethnicity of victims. The additional display of victims increased this effect in accordance with the ethnicity of the depicted victims. When these victims were White, risk estimates for Whites exceeded those for Blacks. When the victims were Black, risk estimates for Blacks exceeded those for Whites. The report version presenting both White and Black victims assumed an intermediate position.

The fact that the seemingly incidental use of ethnicity-defining images was in no way inconsequential for issue perception is perhaps most clearly expressed in Fig. 4.13. The important divergent (White/Black to White) and transverse (White to Black) interactions are obtrusive.

The figure further shows the unexpected effects concerning the risk estimates for Hispanic Americans and for Asian Americans. Neither one of these ethnic groups had been mentioned or image-identified. However, the estimates for these ethnic groups are clearly parallel with those for Blacks, leading to the distressing conclusion that respondents, in this case students and university alumni, rendered assessments along White–Nonwhite lines. The implicit generalization from Black to Hispanic Americans and to Asian Americans was not limited to White respondents, but was also evident in the Black respondents who constituted a minority of only 12% of the respondent pool.

In summary, the findings concerning the effects of incidental pictorial exemplification on issue perception suggest considerable influence. This influence may often be unintended, but it also can be used deliberately to shape the perception of occurrences within the public, especially within the strata of which it is composed. The following generalizations may be offered.

1. The incidental use of image exemplars that add nonredundant, specific information to the text of a report does influence issue perception. Specifically, the "incidental" nature of the pictorial supplementation goes unrecognized and, as a result, is integrated with the narrative information in fostering perceptions and judgment.

2. At present, only short-term effects have been demonstrated. However, as the effects under consideration parallel those of deliberately employed threatening and innocuous images, long-term effects, even sleeper effects, may be considered to be likely.

# FIVE

# Exemplification Effects of Fiction and Quasi-Fiction

· *Correlational Demonstrations*
· *Experimental Demonstrations*

The fact that misrepresentations of exemplified phenomena of interest abound in fiction and in quasi-fiction has been addressed earlier (chapter 2, the section titled "De Facto Exemplification in Fiction and in Quasi-Fiction"). The present question is whether such demonstrable misrepresentations are capable of distorting the perception of these phenomena, thereby creating inappropriate anticipations, dispositions, and ultimately behaviors.

Gerbner and his collaborators (e.g., Gerbner & Gross, 1976a, 1976b; Gerbner, Gross, Morgan, & Signorielli, 1980, 1986) have provided an affirmative answer to this question, insisting that television, as the principal medium of cultural influence, has a global impact on the perception of social reality and that fact–fiction genre distinctions are largely inconsequential, if not entirely irrelevant. It has been argued, for instance, that the news, other reality-type programs, and all fictional formats, as they all tend to dwell on the portrayal of criminal violence, have a joint effect in cultivating a fear of violent crime among the citizenry, thereby fostering the acceptance of protective authority. Such presumed power of undifferentiated television content is thought to impact society on a grand scale. The media have been characterized, in this connection, as "the established religion of the industrial order, relating to governance as the church did to the state in earlier times" (Gerbner & Gross, 1976a, p. 194).

Gerbner and associates (1976a, 1976b, 1980, 1986) have provided correlational data to support their proposal. Specifically, they have separated heavy television viewers (mostly defined as persons watching 4 hours or more daily) from light television viewers (mostly defined as persons watching 2 hours or less daily), and they observed greater apprehensions of becoming a victim of violent crime in heavy viewers as compared to light viewers. Amount of television consumption, then, correlated with fear of crime.

Gerbner and associates (1976a, 1976b, 1980, 1986) gave their findings a causal interpretation in claiming that heavy television exposure *cultivated* the greater crime apprehensions. This circumstance spawned considerable debate among media scholars. For instance, an alternative explanation of the correlation was provided by showing that crime apprehension tends to be high in regions associated with high crime and that people living in these regions are more likely to be heavy viewers, if only because they are more confined to their safe quarters (Doob & Macdonald, 1979; Jackson-Beeck & Sobal, 1980). Other rationales focused on the fact that dramatic fiction not only presents criminal victimization, but also, and perhaps more important, features in its characteristic resolution the curtailment of crime. It was argued that crime-apprehensive viewers might be more strongly drawn to fiction that projects security by showing that criminals are promptly subdued and brought to justice than their less apprehensive counterparts (Zillmann, 1980). This interpretation reverses the causal direction of the observed correlation. Experimental evidence (cf. Zillmann & Wakshlag, 1985) actually provided some evidence for this reinterpretation. The correlation recorded by Gerbner and associates (1976a, 1976b, 1980, 1986) also has been questioned on technical grounds (e.g., Hughes, 1980); among other things, that only extreme social strata were compared (i.e., light vs. heavy viewers) and the midstream of society was not considered. Additionally, more recent experimental work using a prolonged-exposure paradigm generally failed to indicate that the frequent absorption of portrayals of destructive violence would promote fear of bodily mutilation and death, a need for police protection, or punitive eagerness (Zillmann & Weaver, 1997). After extensive exposure to superviolent films, only men scoring high on psychoticism showed increased approval of the death penalty for the commission of heinous crimes. This limited finding might, of course, be deemed consistent with the projection of the media cultivation of fear.

The purpose of the discussion here is not, however, to reopen the debate about the merits of the global media influence proposal as articulated by Gerbner and associates (1986). Assessments of these merits can be found elsewhere (e.g., Morgan & Shanahan, 1997; Potter, 1986, 1993; Zillmann & Wakshlag, 1985). Rather, the purpose is to follow recent investigations in moving from global to more specific media-effects proposals, as well as to express cultivation hypotheses in terms of exemplification paradigms.

The latter is readily accomplished by pointing out that cultivation predictions are based, either implicitly or explicitly, on the massive depiction of particular phenomena in the media and that such massive depiction amounts to high-frequency exemplification of the phenomena in question. Cultivation by the media may be understood, in fact, as the result of the presentation of a vast number of exemplifications of a vast number of phenomena that are culturally relevant. As explicated in the discussion of the interface between direct and mediated experience in chapter 1 (the section titled "The Interface Between Direct and Mediated Experience"), such media influence is bound to interact with the more direct cultivating forces, especially with personal experience attained in immediate social discourse. The indicated interdependencies in the etiology of the individual's perceptions, dispositions, and behaviors are thus marked by a degree of unmanageable complexity that renders the cultivation concept a process label devoid of predictive specificity.

In order to endow the cultivation process with adequate predictive capacity, it seems imperative to abandon global, all-encompassing proposals and to accept the exploration of media influence in specific domains—the results of such explorations being eventually integrable to a comprehensive view of media impact. First and foremost in the initially necessary influence deglobalization is the assessment of the consistency of the media exemplification of the phenomena whose effects are to be discerned. A high degree of variance in the exemplification of a phenomenon is unlikely to foster firm impressions. Consistency across exemplars is a necessary condition for perceptual clarity and stability. Consideration of interference from related but different exemplars, especially from counterexemplars, is equally important. It would be insufficient, for instance, to probe for consequences of frequent portrayals of violence as a means of conflict resolution to focus on the use of overt physical force alone and to neglect the frequency of coercion by threatened force or resolutions by peaceful negotiation. It can be assumed that a degree of such interference is almost always present, which makes its assessment essential for the accurate discernment of media influence.

The suggested neglect of genre differences in the effect of exemplification of phenomena (cf. Gerbner et al., 1980, 1986) also cannot be accepted. As discussed in chapter 1 (the section titled "Exemplification in Different Domains of Communication" and the sections thereafter), it may well be that the format of messages (news, documentary, docudrama, versus the various forms of fiction) goes unnoticed at times or is confused in information-rich media environments by distracted recipients. Such conditions, however, do not apply universally and therefore cannot be assumed to constitute the rule. It would seem prudent, then, to accept, until evidence to the contrary becomes available, that presentational formats are recognized, at least on occasion, and that cognizance of a specific format may influence the degree of credence given to the entailed messages.

As indicated earlier, recent research on the influence of fictional and of quasi-fictional expositions, mostly television programs, has shifted toward greater specificity. Explorations are within formats or genres, but they often provide additional data on the implications of undifferentiated, total television consumption. As our purpose here is to establish that exemplification effects are not limited to the news and to similar reality-based presentations, but that they apply to fiction as well, we review only a sampling of pertinent research. As this work is composed of correlational and experimental demonstrations, illustrations of both approaches are provided.

## CORRELATIONAL DEMONSTRATIONS

Pfau, Mullen, Deidrich, and Garrow (1995) examined the relation between the portrayal of attorneys in prime-time network television programming and the perception of actual attorneys in professional and in private terms. A content analysis was conducted to ascertain the gender and age distributions of featured attorneys, along with other aspects of their existence. One week after the analyzed programs had been aired, a telephone survey of a random sample of households was conducted in the area in which the programs in question could be received. This survey involved the evaluation of actual attorneys on a battery of scales measuring traits such as character, composure, attractiveness, power, presence, and sociability. In addition, estimates of the attorneys' gender and age distributions were obtained. Respondents also estimated their own consumption of prime-time television in hours per week, and they indicated the number of attorney shows they were watching on a weekly basis.

For the incidence estimates of attorneys' gender and age, normative data had been obtained from bar associations. A comparison of television portrayals with viewers' estimates and actual occurrences was thus possible. For instance, the actual proportion of male attorneys was 84%. This ratio was 67% for the depiction of attorneys on television and 71% for the viewers' estimates. Similarly, the actual proportion of young attorneys (up to 36 years of age) was 18%, whereas the ratio for the television depiction was 40% and that for the viewers' estimates 30%. The perception of both the gender and youthfulness of attorneys thus was more closely related to the so-called television answer than to the figures of an unknown reality.

Regarding the evaluation of actual attorneys, significant positive correlations with the amount of attorney-show watching were observed for the traits of character, attractiveness, power, presence, and sociability. The constituent scales of all these traits were oriented such that higher scores indicated more favorable evaluations. The correlations therefore show that the higher the degree of attorney-show consumption, the more favorable the evaluation of actual attorneys—that is, of attorneys outside of television fiction. Did watching attorney drama foster such fortuitous perceptions? Possibly. In view of alternative explanations of the relation under consideration, however, it would be premature to consider a causal relation implicated. A rather compelling alternative explanation is provided, for instance, with the suggestion that viewers who judge attorneys favorably are more strongly drawn to watching programs in which attorneys star than are others.

An investigation by Shrum (1996) focused on the exemplification of social issues in soap operas. Suburban crime and marital discord emerged from content analyses as the prevalent salient topics. The perception of these issues, along with that of the occupational roles of featured characters, was measured in estimates of their prevalence in actuality. Specifically, percentage estimates were solicited by questions concerning, among other things, the relative occurrence of rape and of other violent victimizations for crime, that of loveless marriage and divorce for marital discord, and that of lawyers and doctors for occupational prevalence.

Analogous to the procedures employed by Gerbner and associates (1980), re-spondents were separated into light or heavy viewers, but on the basis of soap-opera consumption instead of total television-viewing time. The segregation was more extreme, in fact, in that selected heavy viewers consumed 5 or more hours of soaps per week and selected light viewers watched no soaps at all.

Amount of soap-opera viewing proved to be correlated with estimates of the prevalence of criminal victimization, of marital discord, and of the highly visible prestigious occupations. The more exposure respondents had to the prevalent themes of soap operas, the higher their estimates of similar occurrences in real life.

A regression analysis that involved numerous control variables (such as grade point average, family income, and need for cognition, but also attention to televi-sion and total viewing time) confirmed these relations. Of particular interest in this is that total television consumption failed to account for the obtained esti-mates to any appreciable degree. The relation between exposure and estimates may thus be considered due to the specific contents of soap operas rather than to watching television at large. To the extent, then, that the observed correlations reflect effects of exposure, such cultivation would be the result of specific exempli-fications, not of exposure to undifferentiated media content.

Shrum's (1996) investigation also involved latency measures for answering the various issue questions. The object of this assessment was to implicate the ease with which constructs under consideration are accessible from memory. Shorter latencies are taken to indicate superior accessibility (cf. Fazio, 1990). If it is argued that in heavy soap-opera viewers the prevalent constructs of soaps are more fre-quently and more recently activated than in nonviewers, shorter latencies in deal-ing with these constructs may be expected. The findings concerning response la-tency are consistent with this interpretation. The argument focusing on the speed of construct accessibility is incomplete, however, in that it fails to explain the dis-tortion in estimation. Ready access may simply reflect familiarity with an issue. It remains unclear how speed of access translates to exaggerated estimates of preva-lence. Is it assumed that interoception of speed of access, should it exist, is precise enough to signal high-frequency manifestation of the phenomenon in question? If so, how could rare occurrences for which ready construct accessibility is estab-lished be perceived as scarce? It would seem to be more plausible to accept a short response latency as a measure of familiarity with a construct and that speedy access does not necessarily carry frequency information with it. It is conceivable, in fact, that the memory search for manifestations of a concept is time consuming and that greater response latencies are associated with issues for which a multitude of exemplars exist.

In considering alternative explanations to the findings of both the prevalence estimates and the response latencies, it can be argued again that viewers who take a liking to high-status protagonists, such as lawyers and doctors, and whose personal experience entails romantic discord, infidelity, deceit, and abandonment, not to mention some risk of criminal victimization, are more strongly drawn to soaps than are viewers without such experiences and predilections. The two groups being compared, soap devotees versus soap ignorers, are simply too different to rule out that what seems to be an effect of exposure may be, at least in part, a consequence of experience-based and disposition-based selective exposure (cf. Zillmann & Bryant, 1985). The latency data, finally, may merely reflect the indicated experiential differences between the two groups.

Davis and Mares (1998), finally, examined the talk-show genre with its admixture of factual and fictitious presentations. The selected social issues, known to be frequently addressed in talk shows, were running away from home, bringing guns to school, teen pregnancy, adultery, and sexual intercourse among teenage boys and girls. Adolescent respondents estimated the relative frequency with which the behaviors subsumed in these issues occurred in reality. They also rated the seriousness of the issues. The estimates and ratings were related to the respondents' consumption of talk shows. This consumption was measured ordinally in four categories: never, rarely, sometimes, and every day.

Regression analysis revealed that incidence estimates were significantly related to the amount of talk-show watching for four out of seven issues. Estimates of teen runaways, teen pregnancies, sexually active males, and sexually active females were clearly related to the amount of talk-show consumption; estimates of teens bringing guns to school, promiscuous husbands, and promiscuous wives were not. The significant relations are obtrusive in the upper four data lines of Table 5.1. As can be seen, estimates are consistently the highest for daily talk-show viewers and are the lowest for nonviewers.

The comparison of estimates with normative percentages, also shown in Table 5.1, further documents the overestimation of the incidence rate by daily viewers. This comparison is compromised, however, by the fact that the estimates of nonviewers also exceed the normative percentages, grossly so, for five of the seven issues. These overestimates by talk-show nonviewers may reflect the frequent exemplification of the issues under consideration in formats other than talk shows, the foremost being broadcast and print news.

Similar to the procedure used by Shrum (1996), a set of control variables were entered into the regression analysis. One such variable was the daily consumption of television irrespective of genre. Corroborating findings reported by Shrum, the amount of total television viewing proved to be unrelated to issue perception—specifically, to incidence estimates concerning various social issues. To the extent that these estimates reflect exposure effects, they would again be the result of exposure to specific content, not to undifferentiated media fare.

TABLE 5.1

Correspondence Between Levels of Talk-Show Consumption and
Incidence Perception Concerning Pertinent Issues in Social Reality

| Estimates in % | Actual % | Talk-Show Viewing | | | |
| --- | --- | --- | --- | --- | --- |
| | | Never | Rarely | Sometimes | Daily |
| Runaway teens per year | 8 | 24.0 | 32.0 | 33.3 | 48.7 |
| Girls getting pregnant before 18 | 4 | 30.0 | 39.8 | 42.0 | 55.1 |
| Boys 15–19 being sexually active | 60 | 59.5 | 69.4 | 72.3 | 79.7 |
| Girls 15–19 being sexually active | 50 | 52.3 | 62.0 | 61.4 | 72.6 |
| Teens bringing guns to school daily | <1 | 21.2 | 28.2 | 25.1 | 26.9 |
| Husbands cheating on their wives | 20 | 38.5 | 45.2 | 43.2 | 45.7 |
| Wives cheating on their husbands | 10 | 26.8 | 30.2 | 34.4 | 31.4 |

*Note.* Estimated percentages differ significantly at $p < .05$ from survey-determined actual percentages, except for those concerning sexually active boys and girls. From "Effects of talk show viewing on adolescents," by S. Davis and M.-L. Mares, 1998 (summer), *Journal of Communication*, 69–86. Adapted with permission.

Davis and Mares (1998) further observed, counter to the expectation that talk shows might trivialize issues, that heavy consumers ascribed greater social importance to some of the issues than did nonviewers. Teen pregnancy, for instance, was deemed a most serious issue by daily talk-show viewers. Should these relations constitute exposure effects, they would manifest talk-show agenda setting, as the more frequent consumption of such shows would increase the salience of presented social issues (McCombs, 1994; McCombs & Shaw, 1972).

Regarding the cultivation proposal (Gerbner et al., 1980, 1986), the findings reported by Davis and Mares (1998) are again open to alternative explanation. It can again be argued that viewers who consider particular social issues highly relevant are more likely to turn to talk shows that address these issues than are viewers who deem the issues less important or irrelevant. It may be the viewers' agenda, then, that brings them to the talk shows—rather than that it is the talk shows' agenda that is adopted by the viewers.

In summary, taken together, the correlational demonstrations of the cultivation of the perception of social issues, along with dependent dispositions and behaviors, may be considered suggestive but not compelling. Causal interpretations of media influence in these terms are exceedingly tenuous, mostly because the findings are readily explained alternatively as the result of selective exposure.

## EXPERIMENTAL DEMONSTRATIONS

Experimental research methods appear to be better suited for the exploration of exemplification effects as the basis of cultivation influences than are correlational techniques, essentially because they entail the random assignment of respondents to controlled exposure conditions. Such assignment eliminates the compromising trait confoundings that accrue to the grouping of respondents by selective, arbitrary criteria. Attributions of effects to specific causes thus can be made with greater confidence.

Regarding cultivation processes, the applicability of experimental methods is severely limited, however. This is because cultivation is conceived of as the result of media exposure to massive amounts of exemplars of particular phenomena. The encounter of a small number of exemplars of any issue is not thought to foster lasting impressions, especially not if it is assumed that a high degree of interference from competing exemplars exists. Experiments in which exposure manipulations amount to varying merely a few exemplars thus can be readily dismissed as failing to simulate the conditions necessary to evaluate cultivation processes. Additionally, such minimal manipulations are unlikely to produce meaningful results. On the other hand, if moderate exemplar variations should yield significant effects, especially nonimmediate ones, the results would be pertinent to cultivation. Experimental research, then, that uses repeated, prolonged exposure to the manifestations of a phenomenon, and that shows effects of such exposure after some delay, may be considered to supplement and expand the evidence concerning the kind of media influence that is subsumed under the cultivation label.

Research employing the indicated prolonged-exposure, delayed-assessment paradigm has been conducted on the effects of pornography consumption on the perception of sexual reality, among other things (Zillmann & Bryant, 1982, 1984). Repeated, prolonged exposure conditions were created by having respondents attend experimental sessions in 6 consecutive weeks. In each session, they viewed either six pornographic films, six control films, or an admixture of three pornographic and three control films. The pornographic films featured consenting adults engaged in all conceivable heterosexual activities devoid of the infliction of pain. The control films were documentaries featuring innocuous themes devoid of sexual or aggressive content. The respondents were then asked, 3 weeks after these exposure treatments, to estimate the incidence rate of various sexual practices of sexually active Americans.

Figure 5.1 summarizes the findings. As can be seen, prolonged consumption of pornography, compared against the control condition, exerted effects on the perception of sex-related reality that persisted for at least 3 weeks. Intermediate exposure resulted in intermediate effects. The consistently strong differentiation of the perceptual exposure consequences observed for the experimental conditions attests to the cultivation of sexual perceptions in accordance with the exemplification of sexual practices in pornography. Essentially, the more exemplars of, for instance, fellatio and cunnilingus had been seen, the higher was the presumed popularity of these oral–genital activities in the populace.

Research conducted within the same exposure paradigm also produced persistent effects of pornography consumption on the perceptions of male and female promiscuity, sexual exclusivity, and the future viability of the institution of marriage (Zillmann & Bryant, 1988a). Moreover, it revealed evaluative effects concerning sexual satisfaction (Zillmann & Bryant, 1988b), dispositional effects concerning sexual coercion (Zillmann & Bryant, 1982), and behavioral effects concerning preferences for sexual themes within pornography (Zillmann & Bryant, 1986).

Hackel (1999), also using the prolonged-exposure, delayed-assessment experimental paradigm, investigated the cultivating effects of talk-show consumption on adolescents' perceptions and dispositions. German high-school students were exposed to talk shows known to be popular in their age group. They attended daily sessions during the course of a week, consuming one program in each session.

The treatment group was exposed to shows dealing with issues considered risqué for that target audience. The control group saw innocuous programs instead. The issues deemed risqué featured the lifestyles of homosexuals and of transsexuals, as well as those of adolescents who embrace body decor by uncommon

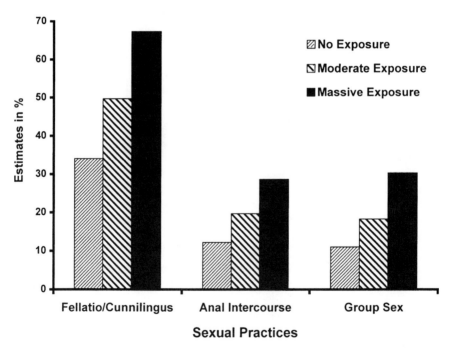

## Pornography Effects on Perception

FIG. 5.1    Incidence estimates of sexual activities practiced by sexually active Americans as a function of no, moderate, or massive exposure to pornography explicitly depicting heterosexual behaviors. Exposure was in weekly sessions during 6 consecutive weeks. Estimates were made 3 weeks after the exposure treatment. Authors' data, from "Pornography, sexual callousness, and the trivialization of rape," by D. Zillmann and J. Bryant, 1982, *Journal of Communication, 32*(4), 10–21.

## Talk-Show Effects on Perception

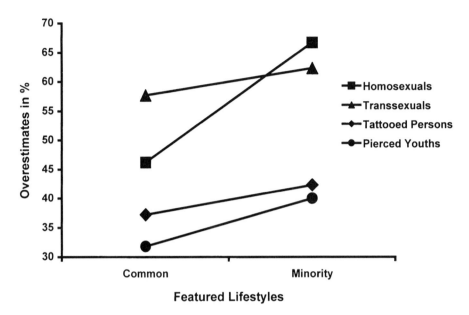

FIG. 5.2    Overestimation of minorities 1 week after a week of daily exposure to talk shows featuring the tacit endorsement of uncommon views and actions by minority members or, in a control condition, innocuous common views and actions by persons not associated with any particular minority. Minority overestimation was assessed through the respondents' choice of an estimate out of a set of provided estimates, one of which was the correct one, the others were either over- or underestimates. The scores reflect the percentage of respondents who selected one of the provided overestimates. From *Die Wirkung von Daily-Talks auf Jugendliche: Eine experimentelle Untersuchung,* by K. Hackel, 1999, unpublished master's thesis, University of Munich, Germany. Adapted with permission.

piercing and tattooing. Hosts, their guests, and members of the immediate audience expressed their approval of the presented lifestyles and decorative preferences. The control group was exposed to themes such as wish fulfillment, moviestar worship, popular fashion, and the election of Miss Germany.

Exactly 1 week after the final exposure session, the respondents were queried about their perceptions of the risqué issues that had been addressed in the treatment programs. Specifically, the respondents estimated the actual incidence rates for persons with minority lifestyles and with decorative preferences as well as the extent to which these minorities are accepted by the general public. Additionally, the respondents indicated their own dispositions regarding the behaviors of the minorities in question.

The findings concerning the incidence estimation of the indicated minorities are summarized in Fig. 5.2. As can be seen, 1 week after exposure to the talk shows,

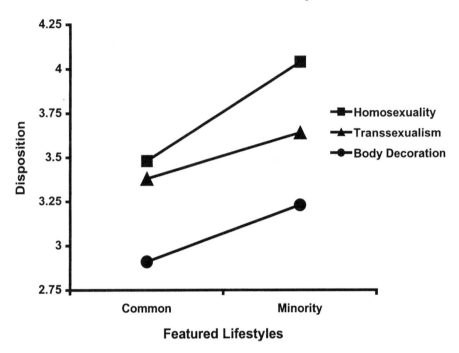

# Talk-Show Effects on Dispositions

FIG. 5.3   Dispositions toward minority lifestyles and preferences 1 week after a week of daily exposure to talk shows featuring the tacit endorsement of uncommon views and actions by minority members or, in a control condition, innocuous common views and actions by persons not associated with any particular minority. Dispositions were measured on a scale ranging from 1 to 5, with scores of 5 indicating the highest degree of acceptance. From *Die Wirkung von Daily-Talks auf Jugendliche: Eine experimentelle Untersuchung*, by K. Hackel, 1999, unpublished master's thesis, University of Munich, Germany. Adapted with permission.

the percentage of all minorities was more strongly overestimated by the experimental group as compared to the control group. This overestimation was most pronounced for the population proportion of homosexuals.

Estimates of the public acceptance of these minorities revealed a significantly greater presumed acceptance for homosexuals only: 27% in the experimental group, compared to 13% in the control. There was no appreciable difference in the presumed acceptance of transsexuals (9% vs. 10%). For persons with body decor (piercing and tattooing combined), the experimental group (31%) showed somewhat greater acceptance than the control group (23%). The difference fell short of significance, however.

Perhaps most important, exposure to approving portrayals of the lifestyles and preferences of minority groups was found to alter the respondents' dispositions toward these groups' behaviors. The pertinent findings are summarized in Fig. 5.3. As can be seen, approving portrayals fostered more favorable dispositions toward homosexuality and body decoration (tattoos and metal adornments through the nose, eyebrows, lips, tongue, nipples, and navel together). Dispositions toward transsexualism were not appreciably affected, however.

These findings can be interpreted as showing the cultivation of tolerance toward minority groups and their behaviors. It should be recognized, however, that such influence is not one of "mere exposure" (cf. Zajonc, 1968), but reflects a favorable, endorsing portrayal of lifestyles and preferences. Contrary influence is to be expected for the debasing and demeaning depiction of the lifestyles and preferences in question.

In summary, sporadic experimentation using a prolonged-exposure, delayed assessment paradigm may be considered to have established that the repeated consumption of fictional and of quasi-fictional media fare can cultivate perceptions of, and dispositions toward, relevant social realities. Such experimentation complements available correlational findings and gives credence to their directional interpretation. The integration of experimental and correlational demonstrations thus provides considerable evidence for the cultivating influence of fiction and of quasi-fiction. The frequent exemplification of not necessarily veridical accounts of circumstances, then, is apparently capable of shaping perceptions and, whenever this exemplification is associated with social approval or condemnation, of modifying behavioral dispositions, bringing them in better accord with seemingly prevalent valuation.

# Toward Exemplification Literacy

- *Exemplification Literacy for Information Providers*
- *Exemplification Literacy for the Citizenry*
- *Closing Remarks*

The fact that acquaintance with exemplars influences the assessment of salient phenomena as well as of comparatively irrelevant phenomena, social and otherwise, should not surprise anyone. For millennia, humans had to render behavior-guiding judgment of general occurrences on the basis of experience with only a limited number of manifestations of these occurrences. The communication of experience eventually broadened the judgmental basis. Integration of personal experience with the experience of others, especially of many others, provided potentially superior grounds for judgment. It also opened the door for misassessment, however, because the conveyance of others' experience could be distorted by the informers' communicative deficiencies or, more likely, by their selfish interest in the matters at issue. Given the severe limitations of personal experience, along with the inevitability of having to act on environments familiar to others but novel to those having to act, there was no alternative to accepting the risk inherent to relying on the not necessarily reliable information provided by others.

In principal terms, this situation has not changed much. Citizens of contemporary society still depend on the conveyance of others' experience, actually more so than in earlier times. As a rule, much of the information needed to exist in today's society exceeds personal experience, and most assessments of societal phenomena have to be formed on the basis of socially transmitted information. The risk that this information is less than reliable can be considered to have grown in leaps and bounds. With the so-called mass media of communication, self-serving distortions and plainly erroneous accounts, whether inadvertent or deliberately created, are multiplied a millionfold.

Surely, it is not suggested here that the media and those controlling these institutions are set on misinforming and misguiding the public. On the contrary, it is assumed that the informational media are committed to providing a reliable accounting of occurrences of relevance. It is to say, however, that erroneous projections occur, often despite good intentions, and that, as they occur, the citizenry is misinformed and misled. Given the magnitude of such effects, the concentration of the dissemination of information pertinent to societal functioning in powerful media institutions can be seen as having not only opened the door, but the flood gates, for the conveyance of misleading information, if not for the occasionally deliberate manipulation of the citizenry. The consequences of the reception of unreliable, nonveridical information are particularly severe, as citizens usually do not have the means to falsify the provided accounts and thus are at the mercy of the informational media.

The entertainment media constitute a special case, of course, in that they are granted poetic license. They need not concern themselves with the veridicality or the typicality of the accounts they feature. The result, to the extent that fictitious accounts are integrated with others in forming impressions of social and of alternative realities (see chapter 5), is that dramatic entertainments are given license to distort, at will, the perception of these realities.

Fiction obviously aggregates case reports irrespective of veridicality and of other limiting considerations. The cases may not be meant to exemplify, but they obviously do so in the minds of readers, of listeners, and of viewers. As they do, they function as exemplars and exert their demonstrated influence on the perception of social reality, in particular.

Exemplars are, no doubt, the lifeblood of fiction. Although less apparent, exemplars also constitute the lifeblood of the news media. Journalistic accounts often concern an individual occurrence that, if it is not entirely atypical and unique, constitutes an exemplar of a broader phenomenon. More characteristic is the aggregation of related exemplars in reports. Such aggregation clearly amounts to exemplification of a phenomenon, whether or not this is explicated. Characteristically, however, phenomena of interest are directly addressed and then are amply exemplified. Without the elaborate display of exemplars, most of journalism would be reduced to the social-science reporting of phenomena with presumably little appeal to its information-seeking clientele. It is the exemplar, the intriguing case report, that is credited with "humanizing" journalism. As this format of storytelling, even when the story relates a general phenomenon, tends to elicit considerable interest, it is the exemplar-laden account that, in the final analysis, sells papers and newscasts. Journalism dedicated to unexemplified, abstract accounts of phenomena, no matter how reliable and effectively informative, has rarely, if ever, been considered a winning formula.

Exemplars not only define the *élan vital* of journalism, they also give journalism its greatest manipulatory power. Considering the outright fabrication of accounts for deliberate deception an illegitimate means that is essentially censored, the aggregation of exemplars lends itself to manipulating, among other things, the perception of public-opinion distributions, the frequency and likelihood of occurrences, and the magnitude of threats and dangers (see chapter 4). Again, it is not suggested that, as a rule, journalists knowingly and deliberately seek to manipulate the public's perception and evaluation of phenomena. Attempts at such manipulation may well be made on occasion. The declared objective, however, is to inform the public about relevant occurrences, thereby providing the basis for informed judgment on the part of the citizenry. The problem is that the journalistic format of apprising the public of relevant occurrences is fraught with manipulatory means of which neither journalists nor citizens are cognizant.

Exemplification may be considered the primary means of this kind. As has been documented (see chapter 2), the use of exemplars permeates communication—informative communication in particular. Journalism relies on exemplification to inform about most, if not almost all, issues of social and societal importance. Being largely ignorant of the consequences of specific uses of exemplars for the assessment of phenomena, journalists may create entirely unintended impressions. Preoccupied with reporting styles, and mostly without concern for the recipients' interpretation of their products, they may, de facto, misinform the public and foster inappropriate reactions—probably with regularity, but at least on occasion.

The citizens are similarly ignorant of the ways in which exemplifications influence their assessment of phenomena, perhaps even more so. They usually have no means of knowing about the wealth of possible exemplars that journalists are likely to have at their disposal and from which, in rather arbitrary fashion, a limited number of exemplars are extracted for display in reports. As citizens have no notion of the relation between all available cases, on the one hand, and the few cases selected for display, on the other, they are defenseless and manipulable because they assume, in good faith, that they are reliably informed about the phenomena that concern them.

Such faith is often unwarranted, however. The recipients' implicit assumption that journalistic accounts present an impartial and unbiased sampling of exemplars of phenomena is rarely justified. Representational accuracy is usually not a criterion that governs exemplar selection. Exemplification thus tends to violate representativeness in both quantitative and qualitative terms. Presentational focus on particular exemplars further exacerbates this inadvertent or deliberate misrepresentation.

Under the premise that accuracy is an objective in apprising the public of relevant social and alternative phenomena, a number of recommendations can be derived from the reported research. First, information providers can be sensitized to the effects that they create by exemplifying in trade fashion that never considered the recipients' processing. Second, recipients can be made cognizant of likely distortions in the journalistic exemplification of phenomena, this in order to allow them to protect themselves against invited misconceptions.

The following constitutes an effort at creating media literacy, specific to exemplification within news reports, in both information providers and consumers. The exemplification concept may, of course, be extended and applied to the selection of phenomena for coverage by the news. This sampling from the uncounted, vast number of phenomena that constitute the environment at large determines what the citizenry gets to know. In other words, it determines the public's attentional focus on issues, thereby giving them salience and inviting contemplation and judgment. Issue selection thus fosters what has been labeled *public consciousness*. The exemplification implicit in this representation of the world's happenings constitutes an issue itself—an issue that demands contemplation and that is too important to be left to unchecked trade practices. However, as this issue lies outside the bounds of the reported research, it will not be addressed here. As stated, all recommendations are specific to within-report exemplification.

## EXEMPLIFICATION LITERACY
## FOR INFORMATION PROVIDERS

Information providers use exemplars under two basic circumstances: when the distribution of particular manifestations of interest in the population is known, or when it is not known. For instance, the distribution of injuries incurred during carjackings has been established and records thereof are accessible; or it has not been ascertained, as in the initial phase of the crime's perpetration.

If the distribution of occurrences is known, the information provider has it as a guide for the unbiased selection of exemplars. Accurate impressions are best achieved by proportional representation of the various manifestations. Such representation is often not feasible, however. Assuming, for instance, that only less than 1% of all carjackings result in the victims' death, reports on the risk of various injuries from carjacking, in order to achieve reliable representation, would have to feature at least 99 nonfatal exemplars in juxtaposition with 1 single exemplar of a carjacking with a fatal outcome. Proportional representation, if not feasible for such practical reasons, should be approached, nonetheless, to the extent that this is possible. If fatal injuries are exceedingly rare, it would be an obvious violation of representational objectives to yield to sensational demands in featuring a majority of exemplars of them while dedicating merely a few to the vast majority of nonfatal cases. A yet more flagrant violation of impartial representation is the practice to exemplify with utterly atypical cases while leaving the majority of cases entirely unexemplified. In such misexemplification, a few gruesome, deadly carjackings would be presented, and they would leave the impression that most, if not all, crimes of this kind are of similar consequence.

Recommendations for information providers, then, are straightforward.

1. In case proportional exemplar representation is possible, it is to be used.

2. In the likely majority of cases in which this is not feasible, it is to be approximated to the degree possible.

3. If the distribution of occurrences involves groupings that are extremely different in size, thus jeopardizing the proportional exemplification of the smallest groupings, it is advisable to represent small groupings by singular exemplars. Such representation amounts to minor overrepresentation and may be questioned. The available evidence suggests, however, that merely making reference to the existence of different but rare occurrences is ineffective in creating correct perceptions.

4. It is advisable to supplement exemplar aggregations with quantitative information about the distribution of occurrences. This applies to ordinally as well as to parametrically structured distributions. It should be recalled, however, that such information serves primarily those with diagnostic interest in reported phenomena and that it is likely to be without appreciable consequence for those to whom the phenomena are less salient.

5. Selective exemplification of rare, atypical occurrences without the accompanying exemplification of substantially different occurrences is inadvisable. Mere reference to the scarcity of the occurrences in focus, to their atypicality, or to the fact that dissimilar occurrences exist neither justifies selective exemplification nor exonerates the users of this common practice. Erroneous perceptions are to be prevented by exemplifying some occurrences that do not meet focal-interest criteria along with the occurrences that are singled out for greater news value or for similar considerations.

6. Using presentational means to achieve superior attention to selected exemplars is inappropriate. It is manipulative, for instance, to feature extensive interviews with parties expressing positions in selective focus while giving short shrift to parties articulating alternative views.

Recommendations concerning the proportional representation of occurrences by exemplars obviously do not apply to situations in which the distribution of occurrences is not known. These situations exist frequently, especially for exploratory ventures into novel occurrences. If nothing is known about the relative frequency of distinct manifestations of phenomena, concepts of proportional exemplification and the typicality of exemplars cannot provide guidance in exemplar selection. Information about the distribution of occurrences may exist and be accessible, however. In such cases, it is incumbent on information providers to attain access and to acquire the necessary knowledge. Only when efforts to that effect prove unproductive and futile are the concepts of representativeness and typicality as well as their implications for exemplification rendered null and void.

This condition does not, however, give information providers license to exemplify arbitrarily, especially under the pretense of knowledge about the incidence rates, trends, and even the typicality of occurrences of interest. Although recommendations (1) through (4) do not apply, recommendation (5) applies in modified form, and recommendation (6) applies in full.

7. In modification of recommendation (5), selective exemplification of occurrences whose relative frequency and typicality are unknown, without the accompanying exemplification of substantially different occurrences, is inadvisable.

8. The recommendation under (6), concerning the inappropriateness of creating superior attention to selected exemplars, applies to occurrences whose distribution is not known as much as it does to quantified distributions.

9. The characterization of selectively exemplified occurrences of unknown incidence as not infrequent, common, or even typical is inappropriate. Information providers must resist using assertions to the effect that reported cases are not isolated occurrences when in fact they are arbitrarily chosen from a distribution about which little, if anything, is known. In this connection, the information providers' personal beliefs of commonness and of typicality are unacceptable in apprising the public of the magnitude of phenomena.

## EXEMPLIFICATION LITERACY
## FOR THE CITIZENRY

The creation of exemplification literacy in the citizenry is particularly important, as only such literacy holds promise of protecting them from forming distorted, erroneous perceptions on grounds of the all-too-often misexemplified projections of phenomena. It is especially important, moreover, because information providers are unlikely to change their practices, even in case of improvement in their exemplification literacy. Journalists tend to think that they are entitled to exemplify at will and without regard to interpretational consequences. They are bound to defend such privileges despite lip service to providing the public with veridical accounts of all phenomena of relevance.

Given the likely reluctance to consider the recipients' information processing and its interpretational consequences, citizens are best advised to hone their own protective skills, especially those regarding the consequences of misexemplification on the perception of issues.

In the most general terms, recipients can be alerted to the fact that information providers have large samples of exemplars at their disposal and that they can pick and choose at will from among these exemplars. This freedom gives them the power to create impressions as they wish. Surely, exemplar aggregates are often chosen in highly responsible fashion. On the other hand, however, the choice usually succumbs to criteria other than veridicality. The selection of exemplar aggregates for presentation is, as a rule, distorted by trade criteria that favor extreme, atypical exemplars. Distorted perceptions, including irresponsibly distorted perceptions, thus are truly invited.

The street-corner interview provides an adequate illustration of arbitrary exemplification. Taking an issue such as the quality of food in the local university's cafeteria, any number of students can be interviewed. A great many different appraisals are the likely result. This gives reporters and editors the opportunity to compose numerous particular exemplifications for their projection of the issue. If they care to be critical of the food services, they can assemble devastating condemnations. On the other hand, if they wish to praise these services, they can compile raving endorsements. Alternatively, they can aggregate any admixture of the two types of patrons' reactions. In other words, they can manipulate exemplifications at will—without the recipients having a chance of detecting the manipulation.

In cases of less variation among pertinent exemplars, the manipulatory possibilities are more limited. Some degree of variance exists, however, for the exemplification of essentially all social phenomena, and this allows manipulatory distortions. Focal interests tend to entail partiality, and this partiality is bound to foster selectivity in exemplifying. Accounts of poverty are thus likely to exemplify the poorest of the poor, accounts of wealth the richest of the rich, accounts of the sick the most grievously ill, accounts of the intelligent the most brilliantly clever, and so on. Analogously, reports on carjackings will feature the most brutal cases and will bypass the less spectacular ones; reports on successful gambling will focus on the lucky winners of many millions of dollars and neglect those with petty-cash earnings; and reports on dissatisfaction at the workplace will single out those threatening to shoot their superiors and ignore the less severely disgruntled.

The indicated selectivity in issue exemplification permeates so-called informative media presentations at all levels. The paradigm of the street-corner interview extends to the opinions of experts and of pundits. For any given issue, editors can readily find opposing views and can aggregate them as they please. Regarding global warming, for instance, any number of doom-projecting experts can be presented. Any number of experts who declare these projections unfounded, untenable, and irresponsible can also be found and presented. The same situation applies to discussions of the need for stricter gun control, the presence of women in the military, the cost of saving endangered species, and perhaps most important, the direction of the economy. In all of these cases, the particular editorial choice of exemplars is bound to determine the perception of the issues by defenseless, uncritical recipients.

A further extension of selective exemplification concerns the choice of specific segments of articulations by public figures. Experts may well qualify their contentions, but qualifications are usually lost in the process of reducing interviews to so-called sound bites. The press, moreover, has the right to rephrase source-attributed statements with impunity—as long as it can be credibly claimed that the interpreter had no defamatory intentions.

The sound-bite reduction is of particular interest in political discourse. In political debates, such as the primaries, positions on salient social issues may be carefully developed and backed by comprehensive argumentation. All of this is likely to be represented by an excerpt of a sentence or two. Reducing articulations to a sound bite for display in the news amounts, of course, to extracting a particular exemplar from a set of possible exemplars. In political discourse, this extraction tends to follow the same distorting choice criteria that have been discussed for other forms of discourse. The likely result is that confrontational excerpts will be featured at the expense of more substantive ones.

All of these considerations lead to the following recommendations.

1. Recipients of informative presentations are advised to be cognizant of the fact that most general phenomena of relevance exhibit considerable variation in individual manifestations, and that this circumstance ensures that information providers have, as a rule, a large sampling of exemplars at their disposal. Most important, recipients are advised to be cognizant of the fact that the extraction of exemplars usually follows trade criteria rather than those of impartial representation. Recipients must be vigilant in recognizing the partiality in exemplifying and must make allowances for this partiality.

2. Recipients are advised to look for quantifications. The quantification of incidence rates concerning phenomena under consideration offers the best corrective for misexemplifications. Such information enables recipients to assess the representativeness and typicality of supplied exemplars. It provides a frame for discerning violations of these criteria.

3. Recipients are advised to treat exemplifications that are not accompanied by information about incidence rates with caution. Such exemplar displays signal that information providers either have no knowledge of the incidence of exemplified occurrences or elected to omit this information in order to exaggerate the significance of the phenomenon.

4. Recipients are advised to exercise caution regarding proclamations of trends or of typicality by assertions such as that reported occurrences would be more and more in evidence or would not constitute isolated cases. Assertions to that effect usually indicate that the incidence rates are not known, even that the cases in question are exceedingly rare.

5. Recipients are also advised to look for presentational distortions. Exemplars given lavish coverage are bound to influence issue perception to a greater degree than hastily acknowledged ones. In particular, recipients should be cognizant of the fact that exemplars capable of eliciting strong emotional reactions tend to exert disproportional influence, and they should guard against any such influence if deemed manipulatory.

## CLOSING REMARKS

To this point, the consideration of possible measures for the correction of often invited erroneous perceptions of issues has concentrated on informative media presentations—on the news in particular. It should not be forgotten, however, that fictional and quasi-fictional presentations are also capable of creating erroneous perceptions through the misexemplification of issues.

For fiction and its kin, it is simply inconceivable that poetic license will ever be challenged and that, for instance, quota would be imposed for the presentation of aspects of issues in the interest of undistorted, veridical perception. In the past, the mere suggestion of voluntary curtailment in the exemplification of destructive behaviors, such as excessively violent actions feared to foster emulation and ultimately to jeopardize public safety, were vehemently rejected as attempts at censorship. As there is little reason to suppose that this stance of the media is likely to change, the burden of correcting misperceptions, even inappropriate dispositions, rests squarely on the recipients' shoulders.

It seems easy enough to advise recipients and recommend corrective measures. All they have to do is to be cognizant of the fictional nature of narratives and then discount them in forming impressions of issues. Such advice is highly cynical, however, because the attentional and judgmental demands of continually separating fact from fiction far exceed the cognitive skills of most who have to cope with rich media environments in which fact and fiction are often intertwined. In addition, the separation requirement is bound to get in the way of the enjoyment of entertainments, and this should greatly diminish any motivation that critical recipients might manage to muster for the task.

It would seem likely, then, that fictional exemplification, especially when set in realistic contexts, will exert some degree of influence on issue perception. This influence may go entirely unchecked for issues of little consequence. It may be speculated, however, that for issues of appreciable personal consequence, recipients will marshal cognitive resources to weigh the evidence at hand and that such scrutiny will result in the discounting of fictional information. The salience of issues is, after all, the condition that also fosters greater attention to information of diagnostic value that is extrinsic to arbitrary exemplar aggregation in nonfictional communication.

# References

Anderson, J. R. (1980). *Cognitive psychology and its implications.* San Francisco: Freeman.

Anderson, J. R., & Bower, G. H. (1973). *Human associative memory.* New York: Winston.

Atkinson, R. C., & Shiffrin, R. M. (1968). Human memory: A proposed system and its control processes. In K. W. Spence & J. T. Spence (Eds.), *The psychology of learning and motivation: Advances in research and theory* (Vol. 2, pp. 89–195). New York: Academic Press.

Aust, C .F., & Zillmann, D. (1996). Effects of victim exemplification in television news on viewer perception of social issues. *Journalism & Mass Communication Quarterly, 73*(4), 787–803.

Axelrod, R. (1973). Schema theory: An information processing model of perception and cognition. *American Political Science Review, 67,* 1248–1266.

Baesler, E. J., & Burgoon, J. K. (1994). The temporal effects of story and statistical evidence on belief change. *Communication Research, 21*(5), 582–602.

Ballstaedt, S.-P. (1977). Eine Inhaltsanalyse zum Filmjournalismus bei "Heute" und "Tagesschau." *Publizistik, 22,* 443–449.

Ballstaedt, S.-P., & Esche, A. (1976). Nachrichtensprache und der Zusammenhang von Text und Bild. *Rundfunk und Fernsehen, 24,* 109–113.

Bandura, A. (1969). *Principles of behavior modification.* New York: Holt, Rinehart & Winston.

Bandura, A. (1971). Analysis of modeling. In A. Bandura (Ed.), *Psychological modeling: Conflicting theories* (pp. 1–62). Chicago: Aldine-Atherton.

Bandura, A. (1986). *Social foundations of thought and action: A social cognitive theory.* Englewood Cliffs, NJ: Prentice-Hall.

Bandura, A., & Barab, P. G. (1971). Conditions governing nonreinforced imitation. *Developmental Psychology, 5,* 244–255.

Bargh, J. A. (1984). Automatic and conscious processing of social information. In R. S. Wyer & T. K. Srull (Eds.), *Handbook of social cognition* (Vol. 3, pp. 1–43). Hillsdale, NJ: Lawrence Erlbaum Associates.

Bargh, J. A. (1996). Automaticity in social psychology. In E. T. Higgins & A. W. Kruglanski (Eds.), *Social psychology: Handbook of basic principles* (pp. 169–183). New York: Guilford.

Bargh, J. A., Chaiken, S., Govender, R., & Pratto, F. (1992). The generality of the automatic attitude activation effect. *Journal of Personality and Social Psychology, 62,* 893–912.

Bargh, J. A., Lombardi, W. J., & Higgins, E. T. (1988). Automaticity of chronically accessible constructs in person situation effects on person perception: It's just a matter of time. *Journal of Personality and Social Psychology, 55,* 599–605.

Bar-Hillel, M. (1980). The base-rate fallacy in probability judgements. *Acta Psychologica, 44,* 211–233.

Bartlett, F. C. (1932). *Remembering: A study in experimental and social psychology.* Cambridge, England: Cambridge University Press.

Berelson, B., & Salter, P. (1946). Majority and minority Americans: An analysis of magazine fiction. *Public Opinion Quarterly, 10,* 168–190.

Bower, G. H. (1992). How might emotions affect learning? In S.-Å. Christianson (Ed.), *The handbook of emotion and memory: Research and theory* (pp. 3–31). Hillsdale, NJ: Lawrence Erlbaum Associates.

Bransford, J. D., Barclay, J. R., & Franks, J. J. (1972). Sentence memory: A constructive versus interpretative approach. *Cognitive Psychology, 3,* 193–209.

Broadbent, D. E. (1958). *Perception and communication.* London: Pergamon.

Brosius, H.-B. (1991). Schema-Theorie: Ein brauchbarer Ansatz für die Wirkungsforschung? *Publizistik, 36,* 285–297.

Brosius, H.-B. (1993). The effects of emotional pictures in television news. *Communication Research, 20*(1), 105–124.

Brosius, H.-B. (1995). *Alltagsrationalität in der Nachrichtenrezeption: Ein Modell der Wahrnehmung und Verarbeitung von Nachrichteninhalten.* Opladen: Westdeutscher Verlag.

Brosius, H.-B. (1996). Der Einfluß von Fallbeispielen auf Urteile der Rezipienten: Die Rolle der Ähnlichkeit zwischen Fallbeispiel und Rezipient. *Rundfunk und Fernsehen, 44*(1), 51–69.

Brosius, H.-B., & Bathelt, A. (1994). The utility of exemplars in persuasive communications. *Communication Research, 21*(1), 48–78.

Brosius, H.-B., Breinker, C., & Esser, F. (1991). Der "Immermehrismus:" Journalistisches Stilmittel oder Realitätsverzerrung? *Publizistik, 36*(4), 407–427.

Brosius, H.-B., Donsbach, W., & Birk, M. (1996). How do text–picture relations affect the informational effectiveness of television newscasts? *Journal of Broadcasting & Electronic Media, 40,* 180–195.

Brosius, H.-B., & Engel, D. (1996). The causes of third-person effects: Unrealistic optimism, impersonal impact, or generalized negative attitudes towards media influence? *International Journal of Public Opinion Research, 8,* 142–162.

Brosius, H.-B., & Mundorf, N. (1990). Eins und eins ist ungleich zwei: Differentielle Aufmerksamkeit, Lebhaftigkeit von Information und Medienwirkung. *Publizistik, 35,* 398–407.

Brosius, H.-B., & Staab, J. F. (1989). Messung und Wahrnehmung politischer Tendenzen in der Berichterstattung der Massenmedien. *Publizistik, 34,* 46–61.

Brosius, H.-B., Staab, J. F., & Gaßner, H.-P. (1991). Stimulusrezeption und Stimulusmessung: Zur dynamisch-transaktionalen Rekonstruktion wertender Sach- und Personendarstellungen in der Presse. In W. Früh (Ed.), *Das dynamisch-transaktionale Modell* (pp. 215–236). Opladen: Westdeutscher Verlag.

Brosius, H.-B., Weaver, J. B., & Staab, J. F. (1993). Exploring the social and sexual "reality" of contemporary pornography. *The Journal of Sex Research, 30*(2), 161–170.

Brown, D., & Bryant, J. (1989). The manifest content of pornography. In D. Zillmann & J. Bryant (Eds.), *Pornography: Research advances and policy considerations* (pp. 3–24). Hillsdale, NJ: Lawrence Erlbaum Associates.

Brown, J. D., & Campbell, K. (1986). Race and gender in music videos: The same beat but a different drummer. *Journal of Communication, 36*(1), 94–106.

Brown, R., & Kulik, J. (1977). Flashbulb memories. *Cognition, 5,* 73–99.

Bruner, J. S. (1951). Personality dynamics and the process of perceiving. In R. R. Blake & G. V. Ramsey (Eds.), *Perception as an approach to personality* (pp. 121–147). New York: Ronald Press.

Bruner, J. S. (1957). On perceptual readiness. *Psychological Review, 64,* 123–152.

Burns, B. (1992). *Percepts, concepts and categories: The representation and processing of information.* Amsterdam: Elsevier Science Publishers.

Cahill, L., Prins, B., Weber, M., & McGaugh, J. L. (1994). ß-adrenergic activation and memory for emotional events. *Nature, 371,* 702–704.

Christianson, S.-Å. (1992). *The handbook of emotion and memory: Research and theory.* Hillsdale, NJ: Lawrence Erlbaum Associates.

Clark, H. H., & Clark, E. V. (1977). *Psychology and language: An introduction to psycholinguistics.* New York: Harcourt.

Collins, A. M., & Loftus, E. F. (1975). A spreading activation theory of semantic processing. *Psychological Bulletin, 82,* 407–428.

Collins, R. L., Taylor, S. E., Wood, J. V., & Thompson, S. C. (1988). The vividness effect: Illusive or illusory? *Journal of Experimental Social Psychology, 24,* 1–18.

Dahlgren, P. (1983). Die Bedeutung von Fernsehnachrichten. *Rundfunk und Fernsehen, 31,* 307–318.

Danks, J. H., & Glucksberg, S. (1980). Experimental psycholinguistics. *Annual Review of Psychology, 31,* 391–417.

Daschmann, G. (1999, May). *Vox pop & polls: The impact of poll results and voter statements on voter judgment.* Paper presented to the Political Communication Division at the Annual Conference of the International Communication Association, San Francisco, CA.

Daschmann, G., & Brosius, H.-B. (1997). Ist das Stilmittel die Botschaft? Fallbeispiele in deutschen Fernsehmagazinen. [Is the style the message? Case reports in German television news.] *Rundfunk und Fernsehen, 45,* 486–504.

David, P., & Johnson, M. A. (1998, Autumn). The role of self in third-person effects about body image. *Journal of Communication,* 37–58.

Davis, M. H. (1983). Measuring individual differences in empathy: Evidence for a multidimensional approach. *Journal of Personality and Social Psychology, 44,* 113–126.

Davis, S., & Mares, M.-L. (1998, Summer). Effects of talk show viewing on adolescents. *Journal of Communication,* 69–86.

Davison, W. P. (1983). The third-person effect in communication. *Public Opinion Quarterly, 47,* 1–15.

Dawes, R. M. (1989). Statistical criteria for establishing a truly false consensus effect. *Journal of Experimental Social Psychology, 25,* 1–17.

Dershowitz, A. M. (1994). *The abuse excuse and other cop-outs, sob stories, and evasions of responsibility.* Boston: Little, Brown.

Dominick, J. R. (1973). Crime and law enforcement on prime-time television. *Public Opinion Quarterly, 37,* 241–250.

Doob, A. N., & Macdonald, G. E. (1979). Television viewing and fear of victimization: Is the relationship causal? *Journal of Personality and Social Psychology, 37,* 170–179.

Driscoll, P. D., & Salwen, M. B. (1997). Self-perceived knowledge of the O. J. Simpson trial: Third-person perception and perceptions of guilt. *Journalism & Mass Communication Quarterly, 74,* 541–556.

Eysenck, M. W., & Keane, M. T. (1990). *Cognitive psychology. A student's handbook.* Hillsdale, NJ: Lawrence Erlbaum Associates.

Fazio, R. H. (1990). A practical guide to the use of response latency in social psychological research. In C. Hendrik & M. S. Clark (Eds.), *Review of personality and social psychology: Vol. 11. Research methods in personality and social psychology* (pp. 74–97). Newbury Park, CA: Sage.

Fiske, S. T., & Taylor, S. E. (1984). *Social cognition.* New York: Random House.

Früh, W., & Schönbach, K. (1982). Der dynamisch-transaktionale Ansatz: Ein neues Paradigma der Medienwirkungen. *Publizistik, 27,* 74–88.

Gan, S., Hill, J. R., Pschernig, E., & Zillmann, D. (1996). The Hebron massacre, selective reports of Jewish reactions, and perceptions of volatility in Israel. *Journal of Broadcasting & Electronic Media, 40,* 122–131.

Gavanski, I., & Roskos-Ewoldsen, D. (1991). Representativeness and conjoint probability. *Journal of Personality and Social Psychology, 61,* 181–194.

Geen, R. G., & Thomas, S. L. (1986). The immediate effects of media violence on behavior. *Journal of Social Issues, 42*(3), 7–27.

Gerbner, G. (1992). Persian Gulf war, the movie. In H. Mowlana, G. Gerbner, & H. I. Schiller (Eds.), *Triumph of the image: The media's war in the Persian Gulf—A global perspective* (pp. 243–265). Boulder, CO: Westview Press.

Gerbner, G., & Gross, L. (1976a). Living with television: The violence profile. *Journal of Communication, 26*(2), 173–199.

Gerbner, G., & Gross, L. (1976b, April). The scary world of TV's heavy viewer. *Psychology Today*, pp. 41–45, 89.

Gerbner, G., Gross, L., Morgan, M., & Signorielli, N. (1980). The "mainstreaming" of America: Violence profile no 11. *Journal of Communication, 30*(3), 19–29.

Gerbner, G., Gross, L., Morgan, M., & Signorielli, N. (1986). Living with television: The dynamics of the cultivation process. In J. Bryant & D. Zillmann (Eds.), *Perspectives on media effects* (pp. 17–40). Hillsdale, NJ: Lawrence Erlbaum Associates.

Gibson, R., Gan, S., Hill, J. R., Hoffman, K., & Seigler, P. (1994). [A content analysis of exemplification in American magazine and broadcast news]. Unpublished raw data.

Gibson, R., & Zillmann, D. (1993). The impact of quotation in news reports on issue perception. *Journalism Quarterly, 70*(4), 793–800.

Gibson, R., & Zillmann, D. (1994). Exaggerated versus representative exemplification in news reports: Perception of issues and personal consequences. *Communication Research, 21*(5), 603–624.

Gibson, R., & Zillmann, D. (1998). Effects of citation in exemplifying testimony on issue perception. *Journalism & Mass Communication Quarterly, 75*(1), 167–176.

Gibson, R., & Zillmann, D. (1999, August). *Reading between the photographs: The influence of incidental pictorial information on issue perception.* Paper presented to the Visual Communication Division of the Association for Education in Journalism and Mass Communication at the national conference, New Orleans, LA.

Ginosar, Z., & Trope, Y. (1987). Problem solving in judgment under uncertainty. *Journal of Personality and Social Psychology, 52*, 464–474.

Good, I. J. (1968). Statistical fallacies. In D. L. Sills (Ed.), *International encyclopedia of the social sciences* (Vol. 5, pp. 292–301). New York: MacMillan & The Free Press.

Graber, D. A. (1984). *Processing the news: How people tame the information tide.* New York: Longman.

Graber, D. A. (1990). Seeing is remembering: How visuals contribute to learning from television news. *Journal of Communication, 40*(3), 134–155.

Greenberg, B. S., Simmons, K. W., Hogan, L., & Atkin, C. (1980). Three seasons of television characters: A demographic analysis. *Journal of Broadcasting, 24*(1), 49–60.

Griffin, D. R. (1984). *Animal thinking.* Cambridge, MA: Harvard University Press.

Grimes, T. (1990). Encoding TV news messages into memory. *Journalism Quarterly, 67*, 757–766.

Grimes, T., & Drechsel, R. (1996). Word–picture juxtaposition, schemata, and defamation in television news. *Journalism & Mass Communication Quarterly, 73*(1), 169–180.

Gunter, B. (1987). *Poor reception: Misunderstanding and forgetting broadcast news.* Hillsdale, NJ: Lawrence Erlbaum Associates.

Gunther, A. C. (1995, Winter). Overrating the X-rating: The third-person perception and support for censorship of pornography. *Journal of Communication*, 27–38.

Gunther, A. C., & Mundy, P. (1993). Biased optimism and the third-person effect. *Journalism Quarterly, 70*, 58–67.

Hackel, K. (1999). *Die Wirkung von Daily-Talks auf Jugendliche: Eine experimentelle Untersuchung.* [The effect of daily talk-shows on adolescents: An experimental investigation.] Unpublished master's thesis, University of Munich, Germany.

Hamill, R., Wilson, T. D., & Nisbett, R. E. (1980). Insensitivity to sample bias: Generalizing from atypical cases. *Journal of Personality and Social Psychology, 39*, 578–589.

Hammerton, M. (1973). A case of radical probability estimation. *Journal of Experimental Psychology, 101,* 252–254.

Haskins, J. B. (1984). Morbid curiosity and the mass media: A synergistic relationship. In J. A Crook, J. B. Haskins, & P. G. Ashdown (Eds.), *Morbid curiosity and the mass media: Proceedings of a symposium* (pp. 1–44). Knoxville, TN: University of Tennessee & The Gannett Foundation.

Hastie, R. (1983). Social inference. *Annual Review of Psychology, 34,* 511–542.

Hayes-Roth, B., & Hayes-Roth, F. (1977). Concept learning and the recognition and classification of exemplars. *Journal of Verbal Learning and Verbal Behavior, 16,* 321–338.

Heider, F. (1958). *The psychology of interpersonal relations.* New York: Wiley.

Heuer, F., & Reisberg, D. (1990). Vivid memories of emotional events: The accuracy of remembered minutiae. *Memory and Cognition, 18*(5), 496–506.

Higgins, E. T. (1989). Self-discrepancy theory: What patterns of self-beliefs cause people to suffer? In L. Berkowitz (Ed.), *Advances in experimental social psychology* (Vol. 22, pp. 93–136). New York: Academic Press.

Higgins, E. T. (1996). Knowledge activation: Accessibility, applicability, and salience. In E. T. Higgins & A. W. Kruglanski (Eds.), *Social psychology: Handbook of basic principles* (pp. 133–168). New York: Guilford Press.

Higgins, E. T., & Bargh, J. A. (1987). Social cognition and social perception. *Annual Review of Psychology, 38,* 369–425.

Higgins, E. T., Bargh, J. A., & Lombardi, W. (1985). Nature of priming effects on categorization. *Journal of Experimental Psychology: Learning, Memory, and Cognition, 11,* 59–69.

Higgins, E. T., & Chaires, W. M. (1980). Accessibility of interrelational constructs: Implications for stimulus encoding and creativity. *Journal of Experimental Social Psychology, 16,* 248–261.

Hill, J. R., & Zillmann, D. (1999). The Oprahization of America: Sympathetic crime talk and leniency. *Journal of Broadcasting & Electronic Media, 43*(1), 67–82.

Hitchcock, A. (1959, July 13). Interview by H. Brean. *Life,* p. 72.

Hoch, S. J. (1987). Perceived consensus and predictive accuracy: The pros and cons of projection. *Journal of Personality and Social Psychology, 53,* 221–234.

Huesmann, L. R., & Eron, L. D. (Eds., 1986). *Television and the aggressive child: A cross-national comparison.* Hillsdale, NJ: Lawrence Erlbaum Associates.

Huff, D. (1959). *How to take a chance: The laws of probability.* New York: Norton.

Hughes, M. (1980). The faults of cultivation analysis: A re-examination of some effects of television watching. *Public Opinion Quarterly, 44,* 287–302.

Iyengar, S., & Kinder, D. R. (1987). *News that matters.* Chicago: Chicago University Press.

Jackson-Beeck, M., & Sobal, J. (1980). The social world of heavy television viewers. *Journal of Broadcasting, 24,* 5–11.

James, W. (1890). *The principles of psychology* (Vol. 1). New York: Henry Holt.

Jo, E., & Berkowitz, L. (1994). A priming effect analysis of media influences: An update. In J. Bryant & D. Zillmann (Eds.), *Media effects: Advances in theory and research* (pp. 43–60). Hillsdale, NJ: Lawrence Erlbaum Associates.

Johnson-Cartee, K. S., & Copeland, G. A. (1991). *Negative political advertising: Coming of age.* Hillsdale, NJ: Lawrence Erlbaum Associates.

Jonides, J., & Naveh-Benjamin, M. (1987). Estimating frequency of occurrence. *Journal of Experimental Psychology: Learning, Memory and Cognition, 13,* 230–240.

Kahneman, D., Slovic, P., & Tversky, A. (1982). *Judgment under uncertainty: Heuristics and biases.* Cambridge, England: Cambridge University Press.

Kahneman, D., & Tversky, A. (1972). Subjective probability: A judgment of representativeness. *Cognitive Psychology, 3,* 430–454.

Kahneman, D., & Tversky, A. (1973). On the psychology of prediction. *Psychological Review, 80,* 237–251.

Kaufman, A., Baron, A., & Kopp, R. E. (1966). Some effects of instructions on human operant behavior. *Psychonomic Monograph Supplements, 1,* 243–250.

Kepplinger, H. M. (1989). Content analysis and reception analysis. *American Behavioral Scientist, 33*(2), 175–182.

Kety, S. S. (1970). The biogenic amines in the central nervous system: Their possible roles in arousal, emotion and learning. In F. O. Schmitt (Ed.), *The neurosciences: Second study program* (pp. 324–336). New York: Rockefeller University Press.

Kintsch, W. (1974). *The representation of meaning in memory.* Hillsdale, NJ: Lawrence Erlbaum Associates.

Kisielius, J., & Sternthal, B. (1984). Detecting and explaining vividness effects in attitudinal judgments. *Journal of Marketing Research, 21,* 54–64.

Kisielius, J., & Sternthal, B. (1986). Examining the vividness controversy: An availability–valence interpretation. *Journal of Consumer Research, 12,* 418–431.

Kissin, B. (1986). *Conscious and unconscious programs in the brain.* New York: Plenum Medical Book Company.

Klatzky, R. (1980). *Human memory: Structures and processes.* San Francisco: Freeman.

Knesset resolution condemns murder. (1994, March 1). *The Jerusalem Post,* p. 5.

Kosslyn, S. M. (1978). Imagery and internal representation. In E. Rosch & B. B. Lloyd (Eds.), *Cognition and categorization* (pp. 217–257). Hillsdale, NJ: Lawrence Erlbaum Associates.

Kosslyn, S. M. (1983). *Ghosts in the mind's machine.* New York: Norton.

Krupat, E., Smith, R. H., Leach, C. W., & Jackson, M. A. (1997). Generalizing from atypical cases: How general a tendency? *Basic and Applied Social Psychology, 19*(3), 345–361.

Landman, J., & Manis, M. (1983). Social cognition. Some historical and theoretical perspectives. *Advanced Experimental and Social Psychology, 16,* 49–123.

LeDoux, J. E. (1992). Emotion as memory: Anatomical systems underlying indelible neural traces. In S.-Å. Christianson (Ed.), *The handbook of emotion and memory: Research and theory* (pp. 269–288). Hillsdale, NJ: Lawrence Erlbaum Associates.

Leo, J. (1994, February 14). Watching "As the jury turns." *U.S. News & World Report,* 17.

Lewicki, P. (1986). *Nonconscious social information processing.* Orlando, FL: Academic Press.

Lyon, D., & Slovic, P. (1976). Dominance of accuracy information and neglect of base rates in probability estimation. *Acta Psychologica, 40,* 287–298.

Mackintosh, N. J. (1974). *The psychology of animal learning.* London: Academic Press.

MacLeod, C., & Campbell, L. (1992). Memory accessibility and probability judgments: An experimental evaluation of the availability heuristic. *Journal of Personality and Social Psychology, 63,* 890–902.

Madigan, S. (1983). Picture memory. In J. C. Yuille (Ed.), *Imagery, memory and cognition: Essays in honor of Allan Paivio* (pp. 65–89). Hillsdale, NJ: Lawrence Erlbaum Associates.

Marks, G., & Miller, N. (1987). Ten years of research on the false-consensus effect: An empirical and theoretical review. *Psychological Bulletin, 102,* 72–90.

Markus, H., & Zajonc, R. B. (1985). The cognitive perspective in social psychology. In G. Lindzey & E. Aronson (Eds.), *Handbook of social psychology* (Vol. 1, pp. 137–230). New York: Random House.

McArthur, L. Z. (1981). What grabs you? The role of attention in impression formation and causal attribution. In E. T. Higgins, C. P. Herman, & M. P. Zanna (Eds.), *Social Cognition: The Ontario Symposium* (Vol. 1, pp. 201–246). Hillsdale, NJ: Lawrence Erlbaum Associates.

McCombs, M. E. (1994). News influence on our pictures of the world. In J. Bryant & D. Zillmann (Ed.), *Media effects: Advances in theory and research* (pp. 1–16). Hillsdale, NJ: Lawrence Erlbaum Associates.

McCombs, M. E., & Shaw, D. L. (1972). The agenda-setting function of mass media. *Public Opinion Quarterly, 36,* 176–187.

McGaugh, J. L. (1992). Affect, neuromodulatory systems, and memory storage. In S.-Å. Christianson (Ed.), *The handbook of emotion and memory: Research and theory* (pp. 247–268). Hillsdale, NJ: Lawrence Erlbaum Associates.

McGaugh, J. L., & Gold, P. E. (1989). Hormonal modulation of memory. In R. B. Brush & S. Levine (Eds.), *Psychoendocrinology* (pp. 305–339). New York: Academic Press.

Meehl, P., & Rosen, A. (1955). Antecedent probability and the efficiency of psychometric signs, patterns, or cutting scores. *Psychological Bulletin, 52,* 194–215.

Mervis, C. G., & Rosch, E. (1981). Categorization of natural objects. *Annual Review of Psychology, 32,* 89–116.

Messaris, P. (1997). *Visual persuasion.* Thousand Oaks, CA: Sage.

Mischel, W. (1968). *Personality and assessment.* New York: Wiley.

Morgan, M., & Shanahan, J. (1997). Two decades of cultivation research: An appraisal and meta-analysis. In B. Burleson (Ed.), *Communication Yearbook, Vol. 20* (pp. 1–45). Thousand Oaks, CA: Sage.

Mundorf, N., Drew, D., Zillmann, D., & Weaver, J. B. (1990). Effects of disturbing news on recall of subsequently presented news. *Communication Research, 17,* 601–615.

Mundorf, N., & Zillmann, D. (1991). Effects of story sequencing on affective reactions to broadcast news. *Journal of Broadcasting and Electronic Media, 35*(2), 197–211.

Navon, D. (1977). Forest before trees: The precedence of global features in visual perception. *Cognitive Psychology, 9,* 353–383.

Neisser, U. (1976). *Cognition and reality.* San Francisco: Freeman.

Nisbett, R. E., Krantz, D. H., Jepson, C., & Kunda, Z. (1983). The use of statistical heuristics in everyday inductive reasoning. *Psychological Review, 90,* 339–363.

Nisbett, R. E., & Ross, L. (1980). *Human inference: Strategies and shortcomings of social judgment.* Englewood Cliffs, NJ: Prentice Hall.

Noelle-Neumann, E. (1980). *Die Schweigespirale: Öffentliche Meinung, unsere soziale Haut.* [The spiral of silence: Public opinion, our social skin.] München: Piper.

Ostrom, T. M. (1984). The sovereignty of social cognition. In R. S. Wyer & T. K. Srull (Eds.), *Handbook of social cognition* (pp. 1–38). Hillsdale, NJ: Lawrence Erlbaum Associates.

Paivio, A. (1971). *Imagery and verbal processes.* New York: Holt, Rinehart, & Winston.

Paivio, A. (1986). *Mental representations: A dual-coding approach.* New York: Oxford University Press.

Paivio, A., Rogers, T. B., & Smythe, P. C. (1968). Why are pictures easier to recall than words? *Psychonomic Science, 11,* 137–138.

Palmgreen, P., Wenner, L. A., & Rayburn, J. D. (1980). Relations between gratifications sought and obtained: A study of TV news. *Communication Research, 7,* 161–192.

Palys, T. S. (1986). Testing the common wisdom: The social content of video pornography. *Canadian Psychology, 27*(1), 22–35.

Pearce, J. M. (1994). Discrimination and categorization. In N. J. Mackintosh (Ed.), *Animal learning and cognition* (pp. 109–134). San Diego, CA: Academic Press.

Perkins, J. W., Jr. (1999). *Effects of information source quantity and personal experience in issue exemplification.* Unpublished doctoral dissertation, University of Alabama, Tuscaloosa.

Perloff, L. S. (1983). Perceptions of vulnerability to victimization. *Journal of Social Issues, 39*(2), 41–61.

Perloff, R. M. (1993). Third-person effect research 1983–1992: A review and synthesis. *International Journal of Public Opinion Research, 8,* 167–184.

Perry, D. K., Howard, T., & Zillmann, D. (1992). Predicting retention of the contents of film drama based upon a fictional or historical context. *Communication Research Reports, 9*(2), 195–203.

Pezdek, K. (1977). Cross-modality semantic integration of sentence and picture memory. *Journal of Experimental Psychology: Human Learning and Memory, 3,* 515–524.

Pfau, M., Mullen, L. J., Deidrich, T., & Garrow, K. (1995). Television viewing and public perceptions of attorneys. *Human Communication Research, 21,* 307–330.

Piaget, J. (1928). *The language and thought of a child.* New York: Harper & Row.

Postman, L. (1951). Toward a general theory of cognition. In J. H. Rohrer & M. Sherif (Eds.), *Social psychology at the crossroads* (pp. 245–272). New York: Harper.

Potter, J. W. (1986). Perceived reality and the cultivation hypothesis. *Journal of Broadcasting & Electronic Media, 30,* 159–174.

Potter, J. W. (1993). Cultivation theory and research: A conceptual critique. *Human Communication Research, 19,* 564–601.

Price, V., Huang, L.-N., & Tewksbury, D. (1997). Third-person effects of news coverage: Orientations toward media. *Journalism & Mass Communication Quarterly, 74,* 525–540.

Price, V., Tewksbury, D., & Huang, L.-N. (1998, Spring). Third-person effects on publication of a holocaust-denial advertisement. *Journal of Communication,* 3–26.

Reyes, R. M., Thompson, W. C., & Bower, G. H. (1980). Judgmental biases resulting from differing availabilities of arguments. *Journal of Personality and Social Psychology, 39,* 2–12.

Rosch, E. (1973). On the internal structure of perceptual and semantic categories. In T. E. Morre (Ed.), *Cognitive development and the acquisition of language* (pp. 111–144). New York: Wiley.

Rosch, E. (1975). Cognitive representations of semantic categories. *Journal of Experimental Psychology: General, 104,* 192–223.

Rosch, E. (1977). Human categorization. In N. Warren (Ed.), *Advances in cross-cultural psychology* (pp. 1–49). London: Sage.

Rosch, E., & Lloyd, B. (Eds., 1978). *Cognition and categorization.* Hillsdale, NJ: Lawrence Erlbaum Associates.

Rubin, A. M., & Perse, E. M. (1987). Audience activity and TV news gratifications. *Communication Research, 14,* 58–85.

Sapolsky, B. S., & Molitor, F. (1996). Content trends in contemporary horror films. In J. Weaver & R. Tamborini (Eds.), *Horror films: Current research on audience preferences and reactions* (pp. 33–48). Hillsdale, NJ: Lawrence Erlbaum Associates.

Sawyer, J. E., Kernan, M. C., Conlon, D. E., & Garland, H. (1999). Responses to the Michelangelo computer virus threat: The role of information sources and risk homeostasis theory. *Journal of Applied Social Psychology, 29*(1), 23–51.

Schaller, M. (1992). Sample size, aggregation, and statistical reasoning in social inference. *Journal of Experimental Social Psychology, 28,* 65–85.

Seggar, J. F. (1977). Television's portrayal of minorities and women, 1971–1975. *Journal of Broadcasting, 21,* 435–446.

Sharkey, J. (1993, December). When pictures drive foreign policy: Somalia raises serious questions about media influence. *American Journalism Review,* 14–19.

Sherman, S. J., Judd, J. M., & Park, B. (1989). Social cognition. *Annual Review of Psychology, 40,* 281–336.

Showers, C., & Cantor, N. (1985). Social cognition: A look at motivated strategies. *Annual Review of Psychology, 36,* 275–305.

Shrum, L. J. (1996). Psychological processes underlying cultivation effects: Further tests of construct accessibility. *Human Communication Research, 22,* 482–509.

Smith, E. R. (1988). Category accessibility effects in a simulated exemplar-based memory. *Journal of Experimental Social Psychology, 24,* 448–463.

Smith, E. R., & Branscomb, N. R. (1987). Procedurally mediated social inferences: The case of category accessibility effects. *Journal of Experimental Social Psychology, 23,* 361–382.

Spear, N. E., & Riccio, D. C. (1994). *Memory: Phenomena and principles.* Boston: Allyn and Bacon.

Spielman, L. A., Pratto, F., & Bargh, J. A. (1988). Automatic affect: Are one's moods, attitudes, evaluations, and emotions out of control? *American Behavioral Scientist, 31*(3), 296–311.

Srull, T. K., & Wyer, R. S. (1980). Category accessibility and social perception: Some implications for the study of person memory and interpersonal judgments. *Journal of Personality and Social Psychology, 38,* 841–856.

Stark, L., & Ellis, S. R. (1981). Scanpaths revisited: Cognitive models direct active looking. In D. F. Fisher, R. A. Monty, & J. W. Senders (Eds.), *Eye movements: Cognition and visual perception* (pp. 193–226). Hillsdale, NJ: Lawrence Erlbaum Associates.

Statistisches Landesamt Baden-Württemberg (Ed., 1996). *Quelle: Amtliche Statistik: Matrialien und Stellungnahmen zur Praxis der Quellenangabe in den Medien.* Stuttgart: Eigenverlag.

Stocking, S. H., Sapolsky, B. S., & Zillmann, D. (1977). Sex discrimination in prime time humor. *Journal of Broadcasting, 21,* 447–457.

Sypher, H. E., & Higgins, E. T. (1988). Social cognition and communication. An overview. *Communication Research, 16,* 309–313.

Tamborini, R., Zillmann, D., & Bryant, J. (1984). Fear and victimization: Exposure to television and perceptions of crime and fear. In R. N. Bostrom (Ed.), *Communication Yearbook 8* (pp. 492–513). Beverly Hills, CA: Sage.

Taylor, S. E., & Crocker, J. (1981). Schematic base of social information processing. In E. T. Higgins, C. P. Herman, & M. P. Zanna (Eds.), *Social cognition: The Ontario Symposium* (Vol. 1, pp. 89–134). Hillsdale, NJ: Lawrence Erlbaum Associates.

Taylor, S. E., & Fiske, S. T. (1975). Point of view and perception of causality. *Journal of Personality and Social Psychology, 32,* 357–368.

Taylor, S. E., & Fiske, S. T. (1978). Salience, attention, and attribution: Top of the head phenomena. In L. Berkowitz (Ed.), *Advances in experimental social psychology* (Vol. 11, pp. 249–288). New York: Academic Press.

Taylor, S. E., & Thompson, S. C. (1982). Stalking the elusive "vividness" effect. *Psychological Review, 89,* 155–181.

Taylor, S. E., Wayment, H. A., & Collins, M. A. (1993). Positive illusions and affect regulation. In D. M. Wegner & J. W. Pennebaker (Eds.), *Handbook of mental control* (pp. 325–343). Englewood Cliffs, NJ: Prentice Hall.

Tedeschi, J. T., Lindskold, S., & Rosenfeld, P. (1985). *Introduction to social psychology.* St. Paul, MN: West.

Tulving, E. (1972). Episodic and semantic memory. In E. Tulving & W. Donaldson (Eds.), *Organization and memory* (pp. 381–403). New York: Academic Press.

Tulving, E. (1983). *Elements of episodic memory.* Oxford: Oxford University Press.

Tversky, A. (1977). Features of similarity. *Psychological Review, 84,* 327–352.

Tversky, A., & Kahneman, D. (1971). Belief in the law of small numbers. *Psychological Bulletin, 76,* 105–110.

Tversky, A., & Kahneman, D. (1973). Availability: A heuristic for judging frequency and probability. *Cognitive Psychology, 5,* 207–232.

Tversky, A., & Kahneman, D. (1974). Judgement under uncertainty: Heuristics and biases. *Science, 185,* 1124–1131.

Tversky, A., & Kahneman, D. (1980). Causal schemas in judgment under uncertainty. In M. Fishbein (Ed.), *Progress in social psychology* (Vol. 1, pp. 5–36). Hillsdale, NJ: Lawrence Erlbaum Associates.

Tversky, A., & Kahneman, D. (1982). Judgement under uncertainty: Heuristics and biases. In D. Kahneman, P. Slovic, & A. Tversky (Eds.), *Judgment under uncertainty: Heuristics and biases* (pp. 3–22). Cambridge, England: Cambridge University Press.

Tversky, B., & Hemenway, K. (1984). Objects, parts, and categories. *Journal of Experimental Psychology: General, 113,* 169–193.

Wanta, W., & Roark, V. (1993, August). *Cognitive and affective responses to newspaper photographs.* Paper presented to the Visual Communication Division at the Association for Education in Journalism and Mass Communication annual conference, Kansas City, MO.

Ward, T. B. (1994). Structured imagination: The role of category structure in exemplar generation. *Cognitive Psychology, 27,* 1–40.

Waugh, N. C., & Norman, D. (1965). Primary memory. *Psychological Review, 72,* 89–104.

White, H. A. (1997). Considering interacting factors in the third-person effect: Argument strength and social distance. *Journalism & Mass Communication Quarterly, 74,* 557–564.

Wilson, T. D., & Capitman, J. A. (1982). Effects of script availability on social behavior. *Personality and Social Psychology Bulletin, 8,* 11–20.

Winterhoff-Spurk, P. (1983). Fiktionen der Fernsehnachrichtenforschung: Von der Text-Bild-Schere, der Überlegenheit des Fernsehens und vom ungestörten Zuschauer. *Media Perspektiven, 10,* 722–727.

Woodall, W. G. (1986). Information-processing theory and television news. In J. P. Robinson & M. R. Levy (Eds.), *The main source: Learning from TV news* (pp. 133–158). Beverly Hills, CA: Sage.

Zajonc, R. B. (1968). Attitudinal effects of mere exposure. *Journal of Personality and Social Psychology, 9,* 1–27.

Zillmann, D. (1980). Anatomy of suspense. In P. H. Tannenbaum (Ed.), *The entertainment functions of television* (pp. 133–163). Hillsale, NJ: Lawrence Erlbaum Associates.

Zillmann, D. (1989). Effects of prolonged consumption of pornography. In D. Zillmann & J. Bryant (Eds.), *Pornography: Research advances and policy considerations* (pp. 127–157). Hillsdale, NJ: Lawrence Erlbaum Associates.

Zillmann, D. (1991). Empathy: Affect from bearing witness to the emotions of others. In J. Bryant & D. Zillmann (Eds.), *Responding to the screen: Reception and reaction processes* (pp. 135–167). Hillsdale, NJ: Lawrence Erlbaum Associates.

Zillmann, D. (1994). Mechanisms of emotional involvement with drama. *Poetics, 23,* 33–51.

Zillmann, D. (1996a). Sequential dependencies in emotional experience and behavior. In R. D. Kavanaugh, B. Zimmerberg, & S. Fein (Eds.), *Emotion: Interdisciplinary perspectives* (pp. 243–272). Mahwah, NJ: Lawrence Erlbaum Associates.

Zillmann, D. (1996b). The psychology of suspense in dramatic exposition. In P. Vorderer, H. J. Wulff, & M. Friedrichsen (Eds.), *Suspense: Conceptualizations, theoretical analyses, and empirical explorations* (pp. 199–231). Mahwah, NJ: Lawrence Erlbaum Associates.

Zillmann, D. (1997). Über die Ikonisierung der Weltanschauung. In Internationales Forum für Gestaltung Ulm (Ed.), *Mensch, Masse, Medien: Interaktion oder Manipulation* (pp. 56–64). Frankfurt am Main, Germany: Anabas Verlag.

Zillmann, D. (1998, October). *Images in the news: Their power to influence information acquisition and issue perception.* Keynote presented at the conference of the Deutsche Gesellschaft für Medienwirkungsforschung, Frankfurt am Main, Germany.

Zillmann, D., & Bryant, J. (1982). Pornography, sexual callousness, and the trivialization of rape. *Journal of Communication, 32*(4), 10–21.

Zillmann, D., & Bryant, J. (1984). Effects of massive exposure to pornography. In N. M. Malamuth & E. Donnerstein (Eds.), *Pornography and sexual aggression* (pp. 115–138). Orlando, FL: Academic Press.

Zillmann, D., & Bryant, J. (Eds., 1985). *Selective exposure to communication.* Hillsdale, NJ: Lawrence Erlbaum Associates.

Zillmann, D., & Bryant, J. (1986). Shifting preferences in pornography consumption. *Communication Research, 13,* 560–578.

Zillmann, D., & Bryant, J. (1988a). Effects of prolonged consumption of pornography on family values. *Journal of Family Issues, 9*(4), 518–544.

Zillmann, D., & Bryant, J. (1988b). Pornography's impact on sexual satisfaction. *Journal of Applied Social Psychology, 18,* 438–453.

Zillmann, D., & Gan, S. (1996). Effects of threatening images in news programs on the perception of risk to others and self. *Medienpsychologie: Zeitschrift für Individual- und Massenkommunikation, 8*(4), 288–305, 317–318.

Zillmann, D, & Gan, S. (1997). Musical taste in adolescence. In D. J. Hargreaves & A. C. North (Eds.), *The social psychology of music* (pp. 161–187). Oxford: Oxford University Press.

Zillmann, D., Gibson, R., Ordman, V. L., & Aust, C. F. (1994). Effects of upbeat stories in broadcast news. *Journal of Broadcasting and Electronic Media, 38*(1), 65–78.

Zillmann, D., Gibson, R., & Sargent, S. L. (1999). Effects of photographs in news-magazine reports on issue perception. *Media Psychology, 3,* 207–228.

Zillmann, D., Gibson, R., Sundar, S. S., & Perkins, J. W. (1996). Effects of exemplification in news reports on the perception of social issues. *Journalism & Mass Communication Quarterly, 73*(2), 427–444.

Zillmann, D., & Paulus, P. B. (1993). Spectators: Reactions to sports events and effects on athletic performance. In R. N. Singer, M. Murphey, & L. K. Tennant (Eds.), *Handbook of research on sport psychology* (pp. 600–619). New York: Macmillan.

Zillmann, D., Perkins, J. W., & Sundar, S. S. (1992). Impression-formation effects of printed news varying in descriptive precision and exemplifications. *Medienpsychologie: Zeitschrift für Individual- und Massenkommunikation, 4*(3), 168–185, 239–240.

Zillmann, D., Taylor, K., & Lewis, K. (1998). News as nonfiction theater: How dispositions toward the public cast of characters affect reactions. *Journal of Broadcasting & Electronic Media, 42*(2), 153–169.

Zillmann, D., Taylor, K., & Lewis, K. (1999). Dispositions toward public issues as determinants of reactions to bad and good news. *Medienpsychologie: Zeitschrift für Individual- und Massenkommunikation, 11*(4), 231–243, 287.

Zillmann, D., & Wakshlag, J. (1985). Fear of victimization and the appeal of crime drama. In D. Zillmann & J. Bryant (Eds.), *Selective exposure to communication* (pp. 141–156). Hillsdale, NJ: Lawrence Erlbaum Associates.

Zillmann, D., & Weaver, J. B. (1997). Psychoticism in the effect of prolonged exposure to gratuitous media violence on the acceptance of violence as a preferred means of conflict resolution. *Personality and Individual Differences, 22*(5), 613–627.

# Author Index

# Subject Index